JAMESTOWN

Timed Readings Plus *in Science*

25 Two-Part Lessons
with Questions for
Building Reading Speed and Comprehension

BOOK 1

Glencoe McGraw-Hill

New York, New York   Columbus, Ohio   Chicago, Illinois   Peoria, Illinois   Woodland Hills, California

JAMESTOWN EDUCATION

Glencoe/McGraw-Hill

A Division of The McGraw·Hill Companies

ISBN: 0-07-827370-6

Send all queries to:
Glencoe/McGraw-Hill
8787 Orion Place
Columbus, OH 43240-4027

2 3 4 5 6 7 8 9 10 021 08 07 06 05 04 03 02

CONTENTS

You probably talk at an average rate of about 150 words a minute. If you are a reader of average ability, you read at a rate of about 250 words a minute. So your reading speed is nearly twice as fast as your speaking or listening speed. This example shows that reading is one of the fastest ways to get information.

The purpose of this book is to help you increase your reading rate and understand what you read. The 25 lessons in this book will also give you practice in reading science articles and in preparing for tests in which you must read and understand nonfiction passages within a certain time limit.

Reading Faster and Better

Following are some strategies that you can use to read the articles in each lesson.

Previewing

Previewing before you read is a very important step. This helps you to get an idea of what a selection is about and to recall any previous knowledge you have about the subject. Here are the steps to follow when previewing.

Read the title. Titles are designed not only to announce the subject but also to make the reader think. Ask yourself questions such as What can I learn from the title? What thoughts does it bring to mind? What do I already know about this subject?

Read the first sentence. If they are short, read the first two sentences. The opening sentence is the writer's opportunity to get your attention. Some writers announce what they hope to tell you in the selection. Some writers state their purpose for writing; others just try to get your attention.

Read the last sentence. If it is short, read the final two sentences. The closing sentence is the writer's last chance to get ideas across to you. Some writers repeat the main idea once more. Some writers draw a conclusion—this is what they have been leading up to. Other writers summarize their thoughts; they tie all the facts together.

Skim the entire selection. Glance through the selection quickly to see what other information you can pick up. Look for anything that will help you read fluently and with understanding. Are there names, dates, or numbers? If so, you may have to read more slowly.

Reading for Meaning

Here are some ways to make sure you are making sense of what you read.

Build your concentration. You cannot understand what you read if you are not concentrating. When you discover that your thoughts are straying, correct the situation right away. Avoid distractions and distracting situations. Keep in mind the information you learned from previewing. This will help focus your attention on the selection.

Read in thought groups. Try to see meaningful combinations of words—phrases, clauses, or sentences. If you look at only one word at a time (called word-by-word reading), both your comprehension and your reading speed suffer.

Ask yourself questions. To sustain the pace you have set for yourself and to maintain a high level of concentration and comprehension, ask yourself questions such as What does this mean? or How can I use this information? as you read.

Finding the Main Ideas

The paragraph is the basic unit of meaning. If you can quickly discover and understand the main idea of each paragraph, you will build your comprehension of the selection.

Find the topic sentence. The topic sentence, which contains the main idea, often is the first sentence of a paragraph. It is followed by sentences that support, develop, or explain the main idea. Sometimes a topic sentence comes at the end of a paragraph. When it does, the supporting details come first, building the base for the topic sentence. Some paragraphs do not have a topic sentence; all of the sentences combine to create a meaningful idea.

Understand paragraph structure. Every well-written paragraph has a purpose. The purpose may be to inform, define, explain or illustrate. The purpose should always relate to the main idea and expand on it. As you read each paragraph, see how the body of the paragraph tells you more about the main idea.

Relate ideas as you read. As you read the selection, notice how the writer puts together ideas. As you discover the relationship between the ideas, the main ideas come through quickly and clearly.

Mastering Reading Comprehension

Reading fast is not useful if you don't remember or understand what you read. The two exercises in Part A provide a check on how well you have understood the article.

Recalling Facts

These multiple-choice questions provide a quick check to see how well you recall important information from the article. As you learn to apply the reading strategies described earlier, you should be able to answer these questions more successfully.

Understanding Ideas

These questions require you to think about the main ideas in the article. Some main ideas are stated in the article; others are not. To answer some of the questions, you need to draw conclusions about what you read.

The five exercises in Part B require multiple answers. These exercises provide practice in applying comprehension and critical thinking skills that you can use in all your reading.

Recognizing Words in Context

Always check to see whether the words around an unfamiliar word—its context—can give you a clue to the word's meaning. A word generally appears in a context related to its meaning.

Suppose, for example, that you are unsure of the meaning of the word *expired* in the following passage:

> Vera wanted to check out a book, but her library card had expired. She had to borrow my card, because she didn't have time to renew hers.

You could begin to figure out the meaning of *expired* by asking yourself a question such as, What could have happened to Vera's library card that would make her need to borrow someone else's card? You might realize that if Vera had to renew her card, its usefulness must have come to an end or run out. This would lead you to conclude that the word *expired* must mean "to come to an end" or "to run out." You would be right. The context suggested the meaning.

Context can also affect the meaning of a word you already know. The word *key*, for instance, has many meanings. There are musical keys, door keys, and keys to solving a mystery. The context in which the word *key* occurs will tell you which meaning is correct.

Sometimes a word is explained by the words that immediately follow it. The subject of a sentence and your knowledge about that subject might also help you determine the meaning of an unknown word. Try to decide the meaning of the word *revive* in the following sentence:

> Sunshine and water will revive those drooping plants.

The compound subject is *sunshine* and *water*. You know that plants need light and water to survive and that drooping plants are not healthy. You can figure out that *revive* means "to bring back to health."

Distinguishing Fact from Opinion

Every day you are called upon to sort out fact and opinion. Because much of what you read and hear contains both facts and opinions, you need to be able to tell the two apart.

Facts are statements that can be proved true. The proof must be objective and verifiable. You must be able to check for yourself to confirm a fact.

Look at the following facts. Notice that they can be checked for accuracy and confirmed. Suggested sources for verification appear in parentheses.

- Abraham Lincoln was the 16th president of the United States. (Consult biographies, social studies books, encyclopedias, and similar sources.)

- Earth revolves around the Sun. (Research in encyclopedias or astronomy books; ask knowledgeable people.)

- Dogs walk on four legs. (See for yourself.)

Opinions are statements that cannot be proved true. There is no objective evidence you can consult to check the truthfulness of an opinion. Unlike facts, opinions express personal beliefs or judgments. Opinions reveal how someone feels about a subject, not the facts about that subject. You might agree or disagree with someone's opinion, but you cannot prove it right or wrong.

Look at the following opinions. The reasons these statements are classified as opinions appear in parentheses.

- Abraham Lincoln was born to be a president. (You cannot prove this by referring to birth records. There is no evidence to support this belief.)

- Earth is the only planet in our solar system where intelligent life exists. (There is no proof of this. It may be proved true some day, but for now it is just an educated guess—not a fact.)

- The dog is a human's best friend. (This is not a fact; your best friend might not be a dog.)

As you read, be aware that facts and opinions are often mixed together. Both are useful to you as a reader. But to evaluate what you read and to read intelligently, you need to know the difference between the two.

Keeping Events in Order

Sequence, or chronological order, is the order of events in a story or article or the order of steps in a process. Paying attention to the sequence of events or steps will help you follow what is happening, predict what might happen next, and make sense of a passage.

To make the sequence as clear as possible, writers often use signal words to help the reader get a more exact idea of when things happen. Following is a list of frequently used signal words and phrases:

until	first
next	then
before	after
finally	later
when	while
during	now
at the end	by the time
as soon as	in the beginning

Signal words and phrases are also useful when a writer chooses to relate details or events out of sequence. You need to pay careful attention to determine the correct chronological order.

Making Correct Inferences

Much of what you read *suggests* more than it *says*. Writers often do not state ideas directly in a text. They can't. Think of the time and space it would take to state every idea. And think of how boring that would be! Instead, writers leave it to you, the reader, to fill in the information they leave out—to make inferences. You do this by combining clues in the story or article with knowledge from your own experience.

You make many inferences every day. Suppose, for example, that you are visiting a friend's house for the first time. You see a bag of kitty litter. You infer (make an inference) that the family has a cat. Another day you overhear a conversation. You catch the names of two actors and the words *scene, dialogue,* and *directing.* You infer that the people are discussing a movie or play.

In these situations and others like them, you infer unstated information from what you observe or read. Readers must make inferences in order to understand text.

Be careful about the inferences you make. One set of facts may suggest several inferences. Some of these inferences could be faulty. A correct inference must be supported by evidence.

Remember that bag of kitty litter that caused you to infer that your friend has a cat? That could be a faulty inference. Perhaps your friend's family uses the kitty litter on their icy sidewalks to create traction. To be sure your inference is correct, you need more evidence.

Understanding Main Ideas

The main idea is the most important idea in a paragraph or passage—the idea that provides purpose and direction. The rest of the selection explains, develops, or supports the main idea. Without a main idea, there would be only a collection of unconnected thoughts.

In the following paragraph, the main idea is printed in italics. As you read, observe how the other sentences develop or explain the main idea.

Typhoon Chris hit with full fury today on the central coast of Japan. Heavy rain from the storm flooded the area. High waves carried many homes into the sea. People now fear that the heavy rains will cause mudslides in the central part of the country. The number of people killed by the storm may climb past the 200 mark by Saturday.

In this paragraph, the main-idea statement appears first. It is followed by sentences that explain, support, or give details. Sometimes the main idea appears at the end of a paragraph. Writers often put the main idea at the end of a paragraph when their purpose is to persuade or convince. Readers may be more open to a new idea if the reasons for it are presented first.

As you read the following paragraph, think about the overall impact of the supporting ideas. Their purpose is to convince the reader that the main idea in the last sentence should be accepted.

Last week there was a head-on collision at Huntington and Canton streets. Just a month ago a pedestrian was struck there. Fortunately, she was only slightly injured. In the past year, there have been more accidents there than at any other corner in the city. In fact, nearly 10 percent of all accidents in the city occur at the corner. This intersection is very dangerous, and a traffic signal should be installed there before a life is lost.

The details in the paragraph progress from least important to most important. They achieve their full effect in the main idea statement at the end.

In many cases, the main idea is not expressed in a single sentence. The reader is called upon to interpret all of the ideas expressed in the paragraph and to decide upon a main idea. Read the following paragraph.

> The American author Jack London was once a pupil at the Cole Grammar School in Oakland, California. Each morning the class sang a song. When the teacher noticed that Jack wouldn't sing, she sent him to the principal. He returned to class with a note. The note said that Jack could be excused from singing with the class if he would write an essay every morning.

In this paragraph, the reader has to interpret the individual ideas and to decide on a main idea. This main idea seems reasonable: Jack London's career as a writer began with a punishment in grammar school.

Understanding the concept of the main idea and knowing how to find it is important. Transferring that understanding to your reading and study is also important.

Working Through a Lesson

Part A

1. **Preview the article.** Locate the timed selection in Part A of the lesson that you are going to read. Wait for your teacher's signal to preview. You will have 20 seconds for previewing. Follow the previewing steps described on page 2.

2. **Read the article.** When your teacher gives you the signal, begin reading. Read carefully so that you will be able to answer questions about what you have read. When you finish reading, look at the board and note your reading time. Write this time at the bottom of the page on the line labeled Reading Time.

3. **Complete the exercises.** Answer the 10 questions that follow the article. There are 5 fact questions and 5 idea questions. Choose the best answer to each question and put an X in that box.

4. **Correct your work.** Use the Answer Key at the back of the book to check your answers. Circle any wrong answer and put an X in the box you should have marked. Record the number of correct answers on the appropriate line at the end of the lesson.

Part B

1. **Preview and read the passage.** Use the same techniques you

used to read Part A. Think about what you are reading.

2. **Complete the exercises.** Instructions are given for answering each category of question. There are 15 responses for you to record.

3. **Correct your work.** Use the Answer Key at the back of the book. Circle any wrong answer and write the correct letter or number next to it. Record the number of correct answers on the appropriate line at the end of the lesson.

Plotting Your Progress

1. **Find your reading rate.** Turn to the Reading Rate graph on page 116. Put an X at the point where the vertical line that represents the lesson intersects your reading time, shown along the left-hand side. The right-hand side of the graph will reveal your words-per-minute reading speed.

2. **Find your comprehension score.** Add your scores for Part A and Part B to determine your total number of correct answers. Turn to the Comprehension Score Graph on page 117. Put an X at the point where the vertical line that represents your lesson intersects your total correct answers, shown along the left-hand side. The right-hand side of the graph will show the percentage of questions you answered correctly.

3. **Complete the Comprehension Skills Profile.** Turn to page 118. Record your incorrect answers for the Part B exercises. The five Part B skills are listed along the bottom. There are five columns of boxes, one column for each question. For every incorrect answer, put an X in a box for that skill.

To get the most benefit from these lessons, you need to take charge of your own progress in improving your reading speed and comprehension. Studying these graphs will help you to see whether your reading rate is increasing and to determine what skills you need to work on. Your teacher will also review the graphs to check your progress.

About the Series

Timed Readings Plus in Science includes 10 books at reading levels 4–13, with one book at each level. Book One contains material at a fourth-grade reading level; Book Two at a fifth-grade level, and so on. The readability level is determined by the Fry Readability Scale and is not to be confused with grade or age level. The books are designed for use with students at middle school level and above.

The purposes of the series are as follows:

• to provide systematic, structured reading practice that helps students improve their reading rate and comprehension skills

• to give students practice in reading and understanding informational articles in the content area of science

• to give students experience in reading various text types—informational, expository, narrative, and prescriptive

• to prepare students for taking standardized tests that include timed reading passages in various content areas

• to provide materials with a wide range of reading levels so that students can continue to practice and improve their reading rate and comprehension skills

Because the books are designed for use with students at designated reading levels rather than in a particular grade, the science topics in this series are not correlated to any grade-level curriculum. Most standardized tests require students to read and comprehend science passages. This series provides an opportunity for students to become familiar with the particular requirements of reading science. For example, the vocabulary in a science article is important. Students need to know certain words in order to understand the concepts and the information.

Each book in the series contains 25 two-part lessons. Part A focuses on improving reading rate. This section of the lesson consists of a 400-word timed informational article on a science topic followed by two multiple-choice exercises. Recalling Facts includes five fact questions; Understanding Ideas includes five critical-thinking questions.

Part B concentrates on building mastery in critical areas of comprehension. This section consists of a nontimed passage—the "plus" passage—followed by five exercises that address five major comprehension skills. The passage varies in length; its subject matter relates to the content of the timed selection.

Timed Reading and Comprehension

Timed reading is the best-known method of improving reading speed. There is no point in someone's reading at an accelerated speed if the person does not understand what she or he is reading. Nothing is more important than comprehension in reading. The main purpose of reading is to gain knowledge and insight, to understand the information that the writer and the text are communicating.

Few students will be able to read a passage once and answer all of the questions correctly. A score of 70 or 80 percent correct is normal. If the student gets 90 or 100 percent correct, he or she is either reading too slowly or the material is at too low a reading level. A comprehension or critical thinking score of less than 70 percent indicates a need for improvement.

One method of improving comprehension and critical thinking skills is for the student to go back and study each incorrect answer. First, the student should reread the question carefully. It is surprising how many students get the wrong answer simply because they have not read the question carefully. Then the student should look back in the passage to find the place where the question is answered, reread that part of the passage, and think about how to arrive at the correct answer. It is important to be able to recognize a correct answer when it is embedded in the text. Teacher guidance or class discussion will help the student find an answer.

Speed Versus Comprehension

It is not unusual for comprehension scores to decline as reading rate increases during the early weeks of timed readings. If this happens, students should attempt to level off their speed—but not lower it—and concentrate more on comprehension. Usually, if students maintain the higher speed and concentrate on comprehension, scores will gradually improve and within a week or two be back up to normal levels of 70 to 80 percent.

It is important to achieve a proper balance between speed and comprehension. An inefficient reader typically reads everything at one speed, usually slowly. Some poor readers, however, read rapidly but without satisfactory comprehension. It is important to achieve a balance between speed and comprehension. The practice that this series provides enables students to increase their reading speed while maintaining normal levels of comprehension.

Getting Started

As a rule, the passages in a book designed to improve reading speed should be relatively easy. The student should not have much difficulty with the vocabulary or the subject matter. Don't worry about the passages being too easy; students should see how quickly and efficiently they can read a passage.

Begin by assigning students to a level. A student should start with a book that is one level below his or her current reading level. If a student's reading level is not known, a suitable starting point would be one or two levels below the student's present grade in school.

Introduce students to the contents and format of the book they are using. Examine the book to see how it is organized. Talk about the parts of each lesson. Discuss the purpose of timed reading and the use of the progress graphs at the back of the book.

Timing the Reading

One suggestion for timing the reading is to have all students begin reading the selection at the same time. After one minute, write on the board the time that has elapsed and begin updating it at 10-second intervals (1:00, 1:10, 1:20, etc.). Another option is to have individual students time themselves with a stopwatch.

Teaching a Lesson

Part A

1. Give students the signal to begin previewing the lesson. Allow 20 seconds, then discuss special science terms or vocabulary that students found.

2. Use one of the methods described above to time students as they read the passage. (Include the 20-second preview time as part of the first minute.) Tell students to write down the last time shown on the board or the stopwatch when they finish reading. Have them record the time in the designated space after the passage.

3. Next, have students complete the exercises in Part A. Work with them to check their answers, using the Answer Key that begins on page 114. Have them circle incorrect answers, mark the correct answers, and then record the numbers of correct answers for Part A on the appropriate line at the end of the lesson. Correct responses to eight or more questions indicate satisfactory comprehension and recall.

Part B

1. Have students read the Part B passage and complete the exercises that follow it. Directions are provided with each exercise. Correct responses require deliberation and discrimination.

2. Work with students to check their answers. Then discuss the answers with them and have them record the number of correct answers for Part B at the end of the lesson.

Have students study the correct answers to the questions they answered incorrectly. It is important that they understand why a particular answer is correct or incorrect.

Have them reread relevant parts of a passage to clarify an answer. An effective cooperative activity is to have students work in pairs to discuss their answers, explain why they chose the answers they did, and try to resolve differences.

Monitoring Progress

Have students find their total correct answers for the lesson and record their reading time and scores on the graphs on pages 116 and 117. Then have them complete the Comprehension Skills Profile on page 118. For each incorrect response to a question in Part B, students should mark an X in the box above each question type.

The legend on the Reading Rate graph automatically converts reading times to words-per-minute rates. The Comprehension Score graph automatically converts the raw scores to percentages.

These graphs provide a visual record of a student's progress. This record gives the student and you an opportunity to evaluate the student's progress and to determine the types of exercises and skills he or she needs to concentrate on.

Diagnosis and Evaluation

The following are typical reading rates.

Slow Reader—150 Words Per Minute

Average Reader—250 Words Per Minute

Fast Reader—350 Words Per Minute

A student who consistently reads at an average or above-average rate (with satisfactory comprehension) is ready to advance to the next book in the series.

A column of Xs in the Comprehension Skills Profile indicates a specific comprehension weakness. Using the profile, you can assess trends in student performance and suggest remedial work if necessary.

Using Energy to Ride a Bike

How do the cereal, milk, and orange juice you had for breakfast help you ride your bike? The food that you eat is fuel for your body. Your body turns this fuel into energy. Your body is always making and using energy.

Just as your body is able to transfer energy from your stomach to your muscles, a bike is able to transfer energy from its pedals to its wheels. The pedals are attached to a cogwheel, which is a wheel with metal teeth. A chain connects this cogwheel with a smaller cogwheel that is attached to the rear wheel. As the larger cogwheel turns, the chain makes the rear cogwheel turn the rear wheel. As the rear wheel begins to turn, the front wheel begins to turn too.

Once you get the bike started, the wheels allow it to roll easily. When one surface rolls over another, the movement causes friction, or resistance, which slows you down. Bike tires are narrow. There is little friction when the small surface of a bike tire rolls across the ground. Bicycle wheels are lightweight. This is because it takes less energy to turn a light wheel than it does to turn a heavy one. Lightweight wheels still have to be strong enough to support the weight of the bicycle and the rider. This is the reason wheels have spokes—to add strength.

Why do you have to pedal harder when going up a hill? You need more energy to overcome the force of gravity. The force of gravity increases as you go up a hill.

When you want to stop your bike, you pull the brake levers. These levers pull cables that move pads against the rim of the wheel. These pads create friction on the rim and slow the wheel down until the bike stops.

Remember to wear a helmet when you ride your bike. If you fall off your bike, you may hit your head. This can cause serious damage to your brain. Most helmets have a hard shell with a layer of stiff foam. The foam can absorb most of the energy of your head's hitting the pavement. Be sure your helmet has a strong strap that will keep it on your head. When you fall off a bike, you may hit your head more than once.

So eat your breakfast, buckle on your helmet, and have a good ride!

Reading Time _____

Recalling Facts

1. Food is fuel that your body turns into
   - ❏ a. muscle.
   - ❏ b. friction.
   - ❏ c. energy.

2. The pedals of a bicycle are attached to
   - ❏ a. a cogwheel.
   - ❏ b. the back wheel.
   - ❏ c. the spokes.

3. You have to pedal harder up a hill because
   - ❏ a. you have to overcome the force of gravity.
   - ❏ b. bike tires are narrow.
   - ❏ c. riding up a hill causes more friction.

4. Brakes slow down a bicycle by using
   - ❏ a. the rear cogwheel.
   - ❏ b. gravity.
   - ❏ c. friction.

5. A helmet helps protect your head in a fall because it
   - ❏ a. uses the force of gravity.
   - ❏ b. absorbs energy.
   - ❏ c. slows you down.

Understanding Ideas

6. You can conclude from the information in this article that
   - ❏ a. your body can change food into the energy needed to ride a bike.
   - ❏ b. riding a bike creates energy.
   - ❏ c. we only use energy when we are exercising.

7. To get energy to play ball after school, you should
   - ❏ a. eat lots of candy.
   - ❏ b. ride your bike.
   - ❏ c. have a healthy lunch.

8. It takes the least amount of energy to ride a bike
   - ❏ a. downhill.
   - ❏ b. uphill.
   - ❏ c. on a level road.

9. The tire that causes the least friction when it is rolling is a
   - ❏ a. bicycle tire.
   - ❏ b. car tire.
   - ❏ c. bus tire.

10. You should wear a helmet
    - ❏ a. only when you ride your bike in the street.
    - ❏ b. every time you ride your bike.
    - ❏ c. only when you ride your bike to school.

Fixing a Flat

My cousin Maria and I were riding our bikes. While we rode, we talked about her problem. She didn't have a topic for her science project. We were swapping ideas when I started running out of breath. At the same time, the ride got bumpy and I slowed down. As Maria shot ahead of me, she said, "Didn't you eat breakfast this morning, Pedro?" Maria likes to tease me.

When I stopped and got off my bike, I heard hissing. The air was leaking out of my back tire! There was a piece of broken glass stuck in it. "Now you're the one with a problem," Maria said. She had come back to check on me.

"Now I know why it was hard to ride. Remember what we learned in science class? When the tire rolls over the road, it causes friction. The more friction, the harder it is to push the wheel. As the air leaked out of my tire, it got flatter."

"So when it got flatter, there was more surface and more friction," Maria added.

We pushed our bikes to the gas station. I got out my patch kit and fixed the tire. When we got back onto our bikes, Maria said, "For my science project, I'm going to show the relationship between air pressure in a bike tire and how much of the tire touches the road."

1. **Recognizing Words in Context**

   Find the word *swapping* in the passage. One definition below is closest to the meaning of that word. One definition has the opposite or nearly opposite meaning. The remaining definition has a completely different meaning. Label the definitions C for *closest,* O for *opposite or nearly opposite,* and D for *different.*

   _____ a. growing

   _____ b. keeping

   _____ c. trading

2. **Distinguishing Fact from Opinion**

   Two of the statements below present *facts,* which can be proved correct. The other statement is an *opinion,* which expresses someone's thoughts or beliefs. Label the statements F for *fact* and O for *opinion.*

   _____ a. Riding a bike is fun.

   _____ b. A bike tire creates friction when it rolls over the road.

   _____ c. As the air leaks out of a tire, the tire gets flatter.

3. Keeping Events in Order

Label the statements below 1, 2, and 3 to show the order in which the events happened.

_____ a. It got harder for Pedro to pedal.

_____ b. A piece of glass got stuck in the tire.

_____ c. Pedro stopped at a gas station and got out his patch kit.

4. Making Correct Inferences

Two of the statements below are correct *inferences,* or reasonable guesses. They are based on information in the passage. The other statement is an incorrect, or faulty, inference. Label the statements C for *correct* inference and F for *faulty* inference.

_____ a. Maria and Pedro like to ride their bikes.

_____ b. Pedro must have run over the glass as he was riding.

_____ c. Friction caused the air to leak out of Pedro's tire.

5. Understanding Main Ideas

One of the statements below expresses the main idea of the passage. One statement is too general, or too broad. The other explains only part of the passage; it is too narrow. Label the statements M for *main idea,* B for *too broad,* and N for *too narrow.*

_____ a. Maria and Pedro often ride their bikes after school.

_____ b. Maria thought of a topic for a science project.

_____ c. Pedro got a flat tire while he was riding his bike.

Correct Answers, Part A _____

Correct Answers, Part B _____

Total Correct Answers _____

Animals of the Forests

Forests provide habitats, or homes, for many animals. There are many different kinds of forests. These include tropical rain forests, temperate rain forests, and deciduous forests.

Tropical rain forests are hot and wet. They are hot because they are near the equator, and they are wet because it rains a lot—more than 250 centimeters (100 inches) per year. Tropical rain forests have tall evergreen trees covered with vines and moss. The tallest trees are known as emergents. Eagles nest here and swoop down to catch a bird or a small monkey from the treetops below.

The canopy, or roof, of the forest is made up of the tops of the tall trees. Fruits, nuts, seeds, and leaves grow here. These things are food for many animals, including bats, parrots, and sloths. Some animals drink water from plants that are shaped like bowls.

Below the canopy is the understory, which is made up of bushes and the lower parts of trees. Here, monkeys with long arms swing from tree to tree. Flying squirrels and frogs glide through tree limbs. Snakes, birds, jaguars, and bugs also live here.

The lowest part of the rain forest is the floor. It is dark and covered with dead plants. Rodents hide in shrubs here. Bigger animals, like the tapir, use their snouts to dig for roots. Thousands of kinds of insects also live in the forest.

Like tropical rain forests, temperate rain forests are wet and have tall trees. Temperate rain forests are found along the western coasts of North America and South America. They are cooler than the tropical forests, and so they have different kinds of plants and animals. Some animals, such as owls and opossums, live in the trees. Others live on the forest floor, including deer, bears, frogs, and skunks. Unlike tropical rain forests, temperate rain forests have one type of tree that is dominant in the area.

Another kind of forest is the temperate deciduous forest. These woods are drier than rain forests. The trees here do not grow as tall. Some animals that live in the temperate rain forest can be found here too. Some of these are deer, bears, and frogs. Rain forests have evergreen trees, but deciduous forests have trees that lose their leaves in the fall. The animals here may have to survive cold winters. Some hibernate. Some birds, such as robins, fly to a warmer place during the winter.

Reading Time _____

Recalling Facts

1. Tropical rain forests are
   - ❏ a. hot and wet.
   - ❏ b. cool and wet.
   - ❏ c. cool and dry.

2. Jaguars live in
   - ❏ a. temperate deciduous forests.
   - ❏ b. temperate rain forests.
   - ❏ c. tropical rain forests.

3. The rain forest canopy consists of
   - ❏ a. shrubs.
   - ❏ b. the tops of the tall trees.
   - ❏ c. the emergents.

4. Temperate rain forests are
   - ❏ a. wet and have very tall trees.
   - ❏ b. found near the equator.
   - ❏ c. hot.

5. Deciduous forests are
   - ❏ a. found mostly along mild coasts.
   - ❏ b. drier than rain forests.
   - ❏ c. habitats for monkeys.

Understanding Ideas

6. You can conclude from reading this article that the different kinds of forests
   - ❏ a. provide different kinds of animal habitats.
   - ❏ b. have the same kinds of animals.
   - ❏ c. are found in the same parts of the world.

7. It is likely that the fruit and leaves on the rain forest floor
   - ❏ a. fell from the trees above.
   - ❏ b. grew on the ground.
   - ❏ c. were planted by humans.

8. It is most likely to snow in a
   - ❏ a. tropical rain forest.
   - ❏ b. temperate deciduous forest.
   - ❏ c. temperate rain forest.

9. You can conclude from reading the article that robins
   - ❏ a. are afraid of possums.
   - ❏ b. live in the same place year round.
   - ❏ c. don't like cold weather.

10. In the rain forest, the water in bowl-shaped plants most likely comes from
    - ❏ a. the plants themselves.
    - ❏ b. rain.
    - ❏ c. dead leaves.

A Listening Walk in the Forest

Gram and Kevin went for a listening walk in the forest. They were quiet as they followed a narrow path through the trees. Soon they heard a long whistle, followed by "to-wit, to-wit, to-wit." High in a tree, Kevin saw a bright red bird. He pointed it out to Gram. She smiled and whispered, "That is a cardinal. See the red crest on top of its head?"

Kevin nodded, and then they went on. Suddenly they heard the snap of a twig and a rustle in the brush. Three deer bounded across the trail, their white tails flicking like flags. "White-tailed deer," Gram murmured.

They continued their walk. The next sound they heard was a small thump near the trail. The noise came again. This time, something dropped from the air right past Kevin's nose and landed at his feet. It was a green nut with a cap on it. Kevin saw it was an acorn. He looked up and saw a squirrel run along a tree branch. "Oak tree," he whispered to Gram.

They walked on and heard a muffled rushing sound. The sound grew louder and louder until finally they came to a creek where a brown mother duck was swimming with her babies. "Mallards," they said in unison. Kevin and Gram sat down to rest on a big flat rock. Kevin wondered what they would hear on the way home.

1. Recognizing Words in Context

Find the word *muffled* in the passage. One definition below is closest to the meaning of that word. One definition has the opposite or nearly opposite meaning. The remaining definition has a completely different meaning. Label the definitions C for *closest*, O for *opposite or nearly opposite*, and D for *different*.

_____ a. loud

_____ b. quiet

_____ c. warm

2. Distinguishing Fact from Opinion

Two of the statements below present *facts*, which can be proved correct. The other statement is an *opinion*, which expresses someone's thoughts or beliefs. Label the statements F for *fact* and O for *opinion*.

_____ a. White-tailed deer are beautiful.

_____ b. Cardinals have crests.

_____ c. Acorns have caps.

3. Keeping Events in Order

Label the statements below 1, 2, and 3 to show the order in which the events happened.

_____ a. Something dropped from the air.

_____ b. Kevin looked up.

_____ c. Kevin saw a squirrel run along a tree branch.

4. Making Correct Inferences

Two of the statements below are correct *inferences,* or reasonable guesses. They are based on information in the passage. The other statement is an incorrect, or faulty, inference. Label the statements C for *correct* inference and F for *faulty* inference.

_____ a. Acorns grow on oak trees.

_____ b. Kevin and Gram liked listening to the forest.

_____ c. Mallards eat acorns.

5. Understanding Main Ideas

One of the statements below expresses the main idea of the passage. One statement is too general, or too broad. The other explains only part of the passage; it is too narrow. Label the statements M for *main idea*, B for *too broad*, and N for *too narrow.*

_____ a. Kevin saw a squirrel.

_____ b. Kevin and Gram took a walk in the woods to listen for animals.

_____ c. Kevin and Gram have gone on long walks together.

Correct Answers, Part A _____

Correct Answers, Part B _____

Total Correct Answers _____

The Constellations

From the beginning of time, people have been watching the sky. Ancient peoples saw that groups of stars appeared in different parts of the sky at different times of the year. Farmers used these groups to tell what season it was and when to plant. People used their imagination to name the groups. They named them for animals, gods, objects, and characters from myths. These groups of stars are called constellations.

One well-known constellation is Orion the Hunter. It can be seen in North America on winter nights. In the southern part of the sky, there are three bright stars in a straight row. These make up Orion's belt. From the belt, other stars extend outward to form a dagger. At the shoulder is a bright star known as Betelgeuse. Orion's left foot is a star called Rigel.

A constellation that is easy to find is Ursa Major, or the Great Bear. The Great Bear can be seen year round in the northern sky. The Great Bear can be seen by first finding the Big Dipper. There are four stars that make up the bowl of the dipper. A line of stars makes up the handle. The bowl of the dipper forms a saddle on the back of the Great Bear. The handle of the dipper is the Great Bear's tail. Before the Civil War, a well-known song called the Big Dipper the Drinking Gourd. Slaves who tried to escape followed the Big Dipper to be sure they were going north.

The two stars at the pouring end of the Big Dipper are called pointer stars. This is because they point to the North Star. The North Star, also called Polaris, is in the same direction as the North Pole. Because of this, sailors and other people who traveled could always find the North Star and use it to tell them which way was north.

The North Star is part of a constellation called Ursa Minor, or the Little Bear. Part of the Little Bear is a group of stars called the Little Dipper. The bowl of the dipper is the Little Bear's side, and the handle is the Little Bear's tail. The North Star is at the very tip of the tail.

There are many more constellations named for animals. There are Orion's dogs, Canis Major and Canis Minor. They hunt Lepus the rabbit and Taurus the bull.

Reading Time _____

Recalling Facts

1. Constellations are
   - ❏ a. winter nights.
   - ❏ b. countries.
   - ❏ c. groups of stars.

2. Ursa Major means
   - ❏ a. dagger.
   - ❏ b. Great Bear.
   - ❏ c. Little Bear.

3. The Drinking Gourd refers to
   - ❏ a. the Big Dipper.
   - ❏ b. Orion.
   - ❏ c. the Little Dipper.

4. Another name for the North Star is
   - ❏ a. Orion.
   - ❏ b. Lepus.
   - ❏ c. Polaris.

5. Lepus and Taurus were named for
   - ❏ a. animals.
   - ❏ b. gods.
   - ❏ c. characters from myths.

Understanding Ideas

6. You can conclude from reading this article that the constellations
   - ❏ a. always stay in the same place in the sky.
   - ❏ b. were of great interest to ancient people.
   - ❏ c. are all found in the northern sky.

7. It is most likely that ancient people named many constellations for animals because they
   - ❏ a. imagined they looked like the animals they knew.
   - ❏ b. didn't like animals.
   - ❏ c. were afraid of the stars.

8. You can conclude from reading this article that the Big Dipper
   - ❏ a. is a very bright star.
   - ❏ b. is part of the Great Bear.
   - ❏ c. was named after a song.

9. You are most likely to find the North Star by
   - ❏ a. following the pointer stars in the Big Dipper.
   - ❏ b. first finding Orion's belt.
   - ❏ c. looking in the bowl of the Big Dipper.

10. It is most likely that Canis Major means
    - ❏ a. Great Dog.
    - ❏ b. Little Rabbit.
    - ❏ c. Big Bull.

| 3 | B | A Visit to a Planetarium |

Yesterday, Ms. Kim's fourth-grade class visited a planetarium. It was a big round room with rows of seats in a circle and a dome overhead. While the class was getting seated, a student asked, "Where are the plants?"

Ms. Kim said, "The word *planetarium* comes from *planet,* not *plant.* We're here to learn about planets and stars." In the center of the room was a large sphere. It was a metal ball that was full of small holes. An amiable man walked in with a smile and started the program, which was called a sky show. He said that the dome was a big screen and the sphere was a star projector. A light in the projector shines through the holes and makes images of stars on the screen.

The room began to darken slowly, as if the Sun were going down. Finally it was very dark and the stars came out. "This is what the sky will look like at ten o'clock tonight," the man said. The students saw the planet Mars, which glowed red. They saw the stars of the Big Dipper and Orion. They learned that because Earth rotates, the stars appear to move across the sky during the night. Then they learned that because of the way Earth orbits the Sun, people see different stars at different times of the year. When the show was over, some students said they were going to look at the stars that night.

1. **Recognizing Words in Context**

    Find the word *amiable* in the passage. One definition below is closest to the meaning of that word. One definition has the opposite or nearly opposite meaning. The remaining definition has a completely different meaning. Label the definitions C for *closest,* O for *opposite or nearly opposite,* and D for *different.*

    _____ a. friendly

    _____ b. mean

    _____ c. smart

2. **Distinguishing Fact from Opinion**

    Two of the statements below present *facts,* which can be proved correct. The other statement is an *opinion,* which expresses someone's thoughts or beliefs. Label the statements F for *fact* and O for *opinion.*

    _____ a. A star projector makes images of stars.

    _____ b. Every class should visit a planetarium.

    _____ c. A planetarium has a dome overhead.

3. Keeping Events in Order

Label the statements below 1, 2, and 3 to show the order in which the events happened.

_____ a. A student said, "Where are the plants?"

_____ b. The students saw the planet Mars.

_____ c. The room began to darken slowly.

4. Making Correct Inferences

Two of the statements below are correct *inferences,* or reasonable guesses. They are based on information in the passage. The other statement is an incorrect, or faulty, inference. Label the statements C for *correct* inference and F for *faulty* inference.

_____ a. You can see plants at a planetarium.

_____ b. You can learn about stars at a planetarium.

_____ c. You can tell what season of the year it is by which stars you can see.

5. Understanding Main Ideas

One of the statements below expresses the main idea of the passage. One statement is too general, or too broad. The other explains only part of the passage; it is too narrow. Label the statements M for *main idea,* B for *too broad,* and N for *too narrow.*

_____ a. The planet Mars glows red.

_____ b. A planetarium sky show teaches students about the night sky.

_____ c. A planetarium provides information about stars and planets.

Correct Answers, Part A _____

Correct Answers, Part B _____

Total Correct Answers _____

The Need for Plants

Imagine a world in which there is no cereal for breakfast, no peanut butter and jelly for lunch, and nothing at all for dinner. There are no hamburgers, fries, or salad. People are not able to meet other basic needs. There are no shirts, jeans, hats, socks, or shoes. There are no cars or planes. This is a world without plants.

All of our food comes from plants. Cereals are made from grains, which are plants. For example, oatmeal is made from oats. Flour, which is used for bread, cakes, and doughnuts, is made from ground wheat. The vegetables we eat, such as carrots and spinach, are plants. Oranges, grapes, and pears are fruits that grow on trees or other plants. Beef and milk come from cows, and cows eat corn and grass. All animals either eat plants or eat other animals that eat plants. So even Thanksgiving turkeys come to our tables, indirectly, from plants.

Our clothes come from plants. Cotton is a plant part that is made into fabric. Cotton is used for jeans, T-shirts, and other clothes. It is also used for towels, sheets, and rugs. Other fabric is made from polyester. Polyester is made from petroleum. Petroleum comes from plants and animals that died millions of years ago and decayed beneath the earth. The buttons on your shirt may be made from tagua nuts, which grow on trees in the rain forest. On the soles of your shoes, you may have rubber that was made from a substance that comes from rubber trees.

Plastic comes from plants. Like polyester, plastic is made from petroleum. Just think of all those ancient decayed plants still hanging around in the shapes of plastic bottles, trash bags, clothes hangers, car parts, garbage cans, and dishes! Rope can be made from plastic or from hemp, which is a plant. Many houses are built of wood from trees. Paper is made from wood pulp. Some paint is made from plant oil.

For centuries, humans have used plants to treat illness. Digitalis is a drug used to treat heart problems. Digitalis comes from a plant called foxglove. Other medicines also are made from plants.

Much of the electricity we use to heat and light our homes is made from burning coal and other fuels, which come from plants. Without plants we would be cold and starving. Without plants, survival would be impossible.

Reading Time _____

Recalling Facts

1. Cereals are made from
   - ❏ a. vegetables.
   - ❏ b. beans.
   - ❏ c. grains.

2. Cotton
   - ❏ a. grows in the rain forest.
   - ❏ b. can be made into fabric.
   - ❏ c. is a kind of polyester.

3. Plastic is made from
   - ❏ a. petroleum.
   - ❏ b. tagua nuts.
   - ❏ c. wood.

4. Digitalis is a kind of
   - ❏ a. plastic.
   - ❏ b. math.
   - ❏ c. medicine.

5. Without plants, we
   - ❏ a. would eat meat.
   - ❏ b. could not survive.
   - ❏ c. would wear polyester.

Understanding Ideas

6. You can conclude from reading this article that beef
   - ❏ a. is not connected with plants in any way.
   - ❏ b. comes from an animal that eats only plants.
   - ❏ c. tastes better than pork chops.

7. You can conclude from the article that
   - ❏ a. plants have been on Earth for a long time.
   - ❏ b. all plants are good to eat.
   - ❏ c. all plants can be made into clothing.

8. It is likely that the clothes you are wearing are made from
   - ❏ a. fabrics that were made from plants.
   - ❏ b. rain forest plants.
   - ❏ c. a tree.

9. You can conclude from reading the article that plastic is
   - ❏ a. made from rubber.
   - ❏ b. used to make many useful things.
   - ❏ c. used to make medicines.

10. You can conclude from reading the article that
   - ❏ a. fruits taste better than vegetables.
   - ❏ b. many kinds of products come from plants.
   - ❏ c. plants grow mainly in forests.

Vegetables from a garden are tastier and more nutritious than the ones sold at a store. Growing vegetables can be fun. You can ask an adult to help you plant them.

Step One: Find the following items: a sunny plot of ground, fertilizer, seeds, a shovel, a rake, a hoe, and water.

Step Two: Decide what to plant and when to plant it. Some vegetables that are easy to grow are tomatoes, beets, and squash. To find out when to plant, look in a garden book, or ask someone who knows a lot about gardens.

Step Three: Prepare the soil. Pull out grass and weeds. Then use a shovel to turn over the dirt and chop up any lumps in the soil. Rake up and remove roots and rocks.

Step Four: Use the hoe to mix fertilizer into the dirt.

Step Five: Plant your seeds in rows. Make a small hole in the ground with your finger. Drop the seed in the hole and cover it with soil. Read the seed packages to see how deep to plant each kind of seed.

Step Six: Water your vegetable garden every day.

Step Seven: As your vegetables start to grow, watch for weeds and pull them out.

Step Eight: Pick your vegetables when they are ripe and ready to eat.

Step Nine: Enjoy!

1. **Recognizing Words in Context**

Find the word *nutritious* in the passage. One definition below is closest to the meaning of that word. One definition has the opposite or nearly opposite meaning. The remaining definition has a completely different meaning. Label the definitions C for *closest,* O for *opposite or nearly opposite,* and D for *different.*

_____ a. crispy

_____ b. full of vitamins

_____ c. unhealthy

2. **Distinguishing Fact from Opinion**

Two of the statements below present *facts,* which can be proved correct. The other statement is an *opinion,* which expresses someone's thoughts or beliefs. Label the statements F for *fact* and O for *opinion.*

_____ a. Beets taste better than squash.

_____ b. You need a sunny area to grow vegetables.

_____ c. Gardeners sometimes pull out weeds.

3. **Keeping Events in Order**

   Label the statements below 1, 2, and 3 to show the order in which the steps should be performed.

   _____ a. Water the vegetables.

   _____ b. Prepare the soil.

   _____ c. Plant the seeds.

4. **Making Correct Inferences**

   Two of the statements below are correct *inferences,* or reasonable guesses. They are based on information in the passage. The other statement is an incorrect, or faulty, inference. Label the statements C for *correct* inference and F for *faulty* inference.

   _____ a. Vegetables can be grown in most backyards.

   _____ b. Vegetable gardens need to be weeded and watered.

   _____ c. You can plant vegetable seeds in the grass.

5. **Understanding Main Ideas**

   One of the statements below expresses the main idea of the passage. One statement is too general, or too broad. The other explains only part of the passage; it is too narrow. Label the statements M for *main idea*, B for *too broad*, and N for *too narrow*.

   _____ a. Vegetables are an important part of a healthy diet.

   _____ b. Tomatoes are easy to grow.

   _____ c. Growing fresh vegetables at home by following some simple steps can be fun.

Correct Answers, Part A _____

Correct Answers, Part B _____

Total Correct Answers _____

5 A What Is a Veterinarian?

A veterinarian is an animal doctor. Veterinarians are also called vets. They treat animals that are sick or hurt and they help healthy animals stay well.

Some vets treat small animals, such as cats, dogs, birds, and hamsters. Many vets who treat small animals work at pet clinics. People bring their pets in to see the vet. Vets give checkups to patients that seem healthy. Suppose the patient is a dog. The vet looks at the dog's hair and skin. This is to check for fleas or skin problems. The vet looks into the dog's ears and checks its teeth. The vet checks the inside of the dog by feeling its organs through the skin.

Vets also teach pet owners how to take care of their pets. Vets keep pets from getting sick by giving them shots or other protective medicine. They clean their patients' teeth and perform surgery. One kind of surgery is to spay or neuter dogs and cats so they can't have unwanted puppies or kittens. Vets also operate to take out tumors. They fix broken bones and mend other injuries.

Some vets treat farm animals. These include horses, cows, sheep, pigs, goats, and chickens. These vets go to farms to see their patients. They must carry all of their supplies with them. They may need to test a herd of cows for disease. They may give a shot to every cow in the herd. They may help a horse give birth to a foal or stitch a cut on a pig's leg. They may even perform surgery in a barn.

Other vets take care of zoo animals. A zoo vet has to treat many kinds of animals. These can include fish, bears, snakes, and seals. Zoo vets might give a zebra a checkup or operate on an elephant. They might clean a lion's teeth or trim a bird's toenails. Before working on large zoo animals, vets first put them to sleep. They do this by shooting darts into their bodies. The darts contain drugs. When the vet is finished working on an animal, he or she gives the animal a shot to wake it up.

It takes years of schooling to be a vet. First, students must take college courses. Then they must go to a school of veterinary medicine and earn a Doctor of Veterinary Medicine degree. All vets have one thing in common. They care about animals.

Reading Time _____

Recalling Facts

1. Veterinarians are
   - ❏ a. farmers.
   - ❏ b. animal doctors.
   - ❏ c. zookeepers.

2. Part of a veterinarian's job is to
   - ❏ a. raise farm animals.
   - ❏ b. treat animals that are sick.
   - ❏ c. walk dogs.

3. Veterinarians spay or neuter cats in order to
   - ❏ a. give them shots.
   - ❏ b. give them a checkup.
   - ❏ c. keep them from having unwanted kittens.

4. Part of a zoo veterinarian's job might be to
   - ❏ a. clean a bear's teeth.
   - ❏ b. give checkups to farm animals.
   - ❏ c. give shots to people's pets.

5. To become a veterinarian, a student must
   - ❏ a. become a Doctor of Veterinary Medicine.
   - ❏ b. visit zoos and farms.
   - ❏ c. own dogs and cats.

Understanding Ideas

6. A vet who treats small animals might
   - ❏ a. give a pet rabbit a checkup.
   - ❏ b. treat a sick cow.
   - ❏ c. help an antelope give birth.

7. You can conclude from reading the article that when a vet gives a dog a checkup, she or he
   - ❏ a. gives the dog a quick look.
   - ❏ b. looks closely at every part of the dog's body.
   - ❏ c. performs surgery on the dog.

8. You can conclude from the information in the article that vets
   - ❏ a. like animals more than people.
   - ❏ b. sometimes save animals' lives.
   - ❏ c. like to visit zoos.

9. It is most likely that vets who treat farm animals carry _____ with them.
   - ❏ a. overalls
   - ❏ b. medicine
   - ❏ c. a saddle

10. A zoo vet is most likely to treat a sick
   - ❏ a. camel.
   - ❏ b. pet cat.
   - ❏ c. chicken.

Are Dogs Getting Healthier?

Dogs are living longer. Twenty years ago, people considered a 12-year-old dog to be very old. Today, many dogs live to be 15 or older. Dogs live 25 percent longer now than they did then! There are two main causes for this change. Dogs eat better food, and they get better health care.

In the 1970s, more people began treating dogs as members of their families. People spent more money to keep their dogs well. Then, other things began to change. Dog-food companies sold more kinds of food for dogs. Puppies, adult dogs, and old dogs need different kinds of food. Some dog foods contain medicines that help prevent diseases.

At the same time, more people began taking their dogs to the vet for checkups. If a problem is found early, it can be treated before it does much damage to the dog. Many dogs used to die from heart disease that was caused by germs from diseased gums. People began to have their dogs' teeth cleaned. More people had their dogs spayed and neutered. Spayed or neutered dogs cannot have unwanted pups. They also are less susceptible to some kinds of cancer. More people stopped letting their dogs run loose. Fewer dogs were hit by cars. New and better medicines were developed. They kept dogs from dying of diseases that used to kill many dogs. Now dog owners can have their best friends with them longer.

1. **Recognizing Words in Context**

   Find the word *susceptible* in the passage. One definition below is closest to the meaning of that word. One definition has the opposite or nearly opposite meaning. The remaining definition has a completely different meaning. Label the definitions C for *closest*, O for *opposite or nearly opposite*, and D for *different*.

   _____ a. acting badly

   _____ b. able to get

   _____ c. protected from

2. **Distinguishing Fact from Opinion**

   Two of the statements below present *facts*, which can be proved correct. The other statement is an *opinion*, which expresses someone's thoughts or beliefs. Label the statements F for *fact* and O for *opinion*.

   _____ a. Puppies need food that is different from adult dog food.

   _____ b. Spayed dogs are less likely to get certain kinds of cancer.

   _____ c. People who let their dogs run loose are stupid.

3. Keeping Events in Order

Label the statements below 1, 2, and 3 to show the order in which the events happened.

_____ a. More people began having their dogs' teeth cleaned.

_____ b. Dogs lived longer.

_____ c. Many dogs were dying from diseased gums.

4. Making Correct Inferences

Two of the statements below are correct *inferences*, or reasonable guesses. They are based on information in the passage. The other statement is an incorrect, or faulty, inference. Label the statements C for *correct* inference and F for *faulty* inference.

_____ a. Dog food tastes better to dogs than it did 20 years ago.

_____ b. More new medicines will be developed for dogs.

_____ c. Dogs that run loose are more likely to get hit by cars.

5. Understanding Main Ideas

One of the statements below expresses the main idea of the passage. One statement is too general, or too broad. The other explains only part of the passage; it is too narrow. Label the statements M for *main idea*, B for *too broad*, and N for *too narrow*.

_____ a. People need to take good care of their pets.

_____ b. Dogs that are spayed or neutered don't get certain kinds of cancer.

_____ c. Dogs are living longer because of better diet and health care.

Correct Answers, Part A _____

Correct Answers, Part B _____

Total Correct Answers _____

The Features of Earth's Surface

The surface of Earth is wrinkled with mountains and carved out with valleys. In some places the surface is flat. Earth is crossed by rivers and dotted with lakes. Much of it is covered by ocean.

All of Earth's land and ocean sit on a layer of rock. This layer is called the lithosphere. The lithosphere is made up of sections called plates. Large cracks between plates are called faults. Plates move because of pressure from deep within Earth. When plates press against each other, they can push up layers of rock, which is how some mountains are created. When plates move apart, they can cause large blocks of Earth's surface to sink.

Other mountains are made by volcanoes. Melted rock called magma moves up from deep inside Earth. As it rises, it gives off gases. These gases push on Earth's surface and cause it to bulge. When the pressure gets very high, the gas explodes out of the ground. The magma that comes out of the volcano is called lava. The volcano erupts again and again, and the lava builds up to form a mountain. Sometimes many years pass between eruptions.

Land can also be shaped by erosion. Erosion occurs when water or wind wears away softer rock and leaves behind harder rock. After a long, long time, the harder rock may stand alone as mountains. Sometimes it appears as the walls of canyons.

Water moves from high ground to low ground. Small streams can come together to form large streams. Large streams can join to form rivers. Rivers flow into lakes or the ocean.

The ocean is a huge body of salt water that covers almost three-fourths of Earth. The ocean is divided into smaller oceans and seas. On the ocean floor are the midocean ridges. These are chains of mountains formed by volcanoes. There are many large cracks between the ridges. As some of the cracks widen, magma comes up and forms new mountains. Many islands are volcanoes that have risen above the surface of the ocean. Hawaii was formed this way.

The surface of Earth is always changing. At one time, all land was in one place. The ocean covered the rest of the world. As the plates slowly moved, the land broke apart. Ocean water moved between the masses of land. Over a long period of time, the continents we know today were formed.

Reading Time _____

Recalling Facts

1. The lithosphere is
   - ❏ a. the bottom of the ocean.
   - ❏ b. a layer of rock.
   - ❏ c. a volcano.

2. The lithosphere is made up of
   - ❏ a. lava.
   - ❏ b. mountains.
   - ❏ c. plates.

3. Magma is
   - ❏ a. melted rock.
   - ❏ b. erosion.
   - ❏ c. salt water.

4. The ocean covers about _____ of Earth's surface.
   - ❏ a. half
   - ❏ b. three-fourths
   - ❏ c. one-fourth

5. The midocean ridges
   - ❏ a. are mountains under the ocean.
   - ❏ b. were formed by erosion.
   - ❏ c. are crossed by rivers.

Understanding Ideas

6. You can conclude from reading this article that Earth's surface
   - ❏ a. is the same everywhere.
   - ❏ b. is sinking.
   - ❏ c. has many different features.

7. Mountains are most likely to form
   - ❏ a. along faults.
   - ❏ b. in the middle of a plate.
   - ❏ c. next to streams.

8. You can conclude from reading the article that erosion can
   - ❏ a. form a mountain.
   - ❏ b. cause a volcano to erupt.
   - ❏ c. make new rock.

9. You can conclude that
   - ❏ a. there is more land than ocean on Earth.
   - ❏ b. the ocean will someday cover all the land.
   - ❏ c. there is more ocean than land on Earth.

10. You can conclude that
    - ❏ a. the surface of Earth will continue to change.
    - ❏ b. the continents will stay where they are forever.
    - ❏ c. volcanoes don't change Earth's surface.

Down the Mississippi River

Last summer, my family took a river trip down the Mississippi. The river starts out as a small creek that flows from a lake in Minnesota. We began our trip at St. Paul, the capital of Minnesota. There the river is wide enough for bigger boats. After we left St. Paul, we saw some cormorants. These are birds that eat fish and swim. While Mom watched them dive for fish, Dad saw an eagle.

Farther south, we saw a sign on the riverbank where Minnesota, Iowa, and Wisconsin meet. As we went on, we saw islands and sandbars. The river has lots of twists and turns. It widened as we went farther south. This is because more rivers merge with it. Also, it collects water that runs off the land. One day, we saw a tugboat pushing 15 barges. Barges are flat ships that carry goods. Later on we saw tugs with 50 barges. Once, when we were south of Baton Rouge, Louisiana, we saw ocean ships on the river. As we got close to New Orleans, I saw two alligators.

Our trip ended in New Orleans, but the Mississippi River runs on to the Gulf of Mexico. The river is more than 3,200 kilometers (2,000 miles) long. It flows along the borders of 10 states!

1. **Recognizing Words in Context**

   Find the word *merge* in the passage. One definition below is closest to the meaning of that word. One definition has the opposite or nearly opposite meaning. The remaining definition has a completely different meaning. Label the definitions C for *closest,* O *for opposite or nearly opposite,* and D for *different.*

   _____ a. want

   _____ b. combine

   _____ c. divide

2. **Distinguishing Fact from Opinion**

   Two of the statements below present *facts,* which can be proved correct. The other statement is an *opinion,* which expresses someone's thoughts or beliefs. Label the statements F for *fact* and O for *opinion.*

   _____ a. The Mississippi River is more than 3,200 kilometers long.

   _____ b. A tug can push 50 barges.

   _____ c. Ocean ships should not travel on rivers.

3. **Keeping Events in Order**

   Label the statements below 1, 2, and 3 to show the order in which the events happened.

   _____ a. The full barges were pushed up the Mississippi by a tugboat.

   _____ b. Farmers harvested corn.

   _____ c. The corn was loaded onto barges.

4. **Making Correct Inferences**

   Two of the statements below are correct *inferences,* or reasonable guesses. They are based on information in the passage. The other statement is an incorrect, or faulty, inference. Label the statements C for *correct* inference and F for *faulty* inference.

   _____ a. The Mississippi is a very long river.

   _____ b. The Mississippi River is wider at New Orleans than it is at St. Paul.

   _____ c. The Mississippi River ends at New Orleans.

5. **Understanding Main Ideas**

   One of the statements below expresses the main idea of the passage. One statement is too general, or too broad. The other explains only part of the passage; it is too narrow. Label the statements M for *main idea*, B for *too broad,* and N for *too narrow.*

   _____ a. The Mississippi has lots of twists and turns.

   _____ b. There is much to see on a trip down the Mississippi River.

   _____ c. The United States has several long rivers.

Correct Answers, Part A _____

Correct Answers, Part B _____

Total Correct Answers _____

Simple Machines

A machine is a device that helps people to do more work than they can do by themselves. When you think of a machine, you probably think of something that has many parts. But some machines have only one or two parts. These are called simple machines. Simple machines make it easier to move heavy objects. Some of the most common simple machines are levers, pulleys, and inclined planes.

A lever is a rod. When using a lever, a person transfers a force from one end of the rod to the other. This is done by putting the rod on a fulcrum, which is a point that stays still. One kind of lever is a seesaw. Here the fulcrum is in the middle. A seat is at each end of the rod. When you push down on one end, you raise the weight on the other end. If the lever has a fulcrum that is close to one end, only a small amount of force is needed at the other end to move the object. Another common example of a lever is a crowbar.

A pulley is a wheel that turns on an axle. The wheel has a groove cut in its edge. A rope runs through the groove. The wheel of the pulley turns when the rope is pulled.

Pulleys are usually attached to high places, such as a wooden beam on the ceiling of a warehouse. A person ties one end of the rope around a heavy object and pulls on the other end. The wheel changes the direction of the force that is created when the person pulls on the rope. The pulley makes it easier to lift the object, because it is easier to pull down on a rope with a heavy load than to pull the load up.

An inclined plane is a straight, slanted surface, such as a ramp. It is easier to push an object up a ramp than it is to lift an object straight up in the air. The longer the ramp, the easier it is to move the object. This is because the pull of gravity is stronger against something moving straight up than it is against something moving diagonally on a ramp. Another example of an inclined plane is a road that runs uphill. The steeper the road, the more difficult it is to walk up.

Reading Time _____

Recalling Facts

1. A lever is
   - ❏ a. a simple machine.
   - ❏ b. a compound machine.
   - ❏ c. an inclined plane.

2. A seesaw is a
   - ❏ a. load.
   - ❏ b. pulley.
   - ❏ c. lever.

3. A pulley has
   - ❏ a. an inclined plane on a fulcrum.
   - ❏ b. a wheel that turns on an axle.
   - ❏ c. a lever on a rope.

4. A ramp is
   - ❏ a. an inclined plane.
   - ❏ b. a fulcrum.
   - ❏ c. a lever.

5. A road on a hill is
   - ❏ a. a lever.
   - ❏ b. an inclined plane.
   - ❏ c. a pulley.

Understanding Ideas

6. You can conclude from reading this article that simple machines
   - ❏ a. are made of many different parts.
   - ❏ b. can help you work faster.
   - ❏ c. require only a small amount of electricity.

7. If you want to move a big rock that is stuck in the ground, you would most likely use
   - ❏ a. an inclined plane.
   - ❏ b. a lever.
   - ❏ c. a pulley.

8. If you want to move a wheelbarrow filled with dirt up some steps, you could create a _____ by putting a wide board over the steps.
   - ❏ a. ramp
   - ❏ b. pulley
   - ❏ c. lever

9. You can conclude from reading the article that simple machines are
   - ❏ a. all around us.
   - ❏ b. hard to find.
   - ❏ c. difficult to use.

10. You can conclude that a crowbar is a
    - ❏ a. simple machine.
    - ❏ b. power tool.
    - ❏ c. fulcrum.

A Simple Solution

Tony and Jennifer sat on the floor of their tree house playing cards. Jennifer said, "I wish we had some chairs."

"We could get those two big beanbag chairs in the basement," Tony suggested.

Jennifer looked out the window and down at the ground. She said, "We can't carry them while we climb up here." They decided to pull the chairs up with a rope.

Jennifer went to find a long rope while Tony got the chairs. They tied the rope around one of the chairs. They took the other end of the rope and climbed up to the tree house. They tugged on the rope, but it was very hard to hoist the chair. When the chair was only halfway up, their arms got tired, and they had to let go of the rope. Then Jennifer remembered seeing a pulley on their dad's workbench. Their dad brought a ladder and attached the pulley to the tree house, just above the window. Jennifer threaded the rope around the pulley.

On the ground, Tony tied one end of the rope to a chair. He pulled on the other end of the rope. It was easy to lift the chair. When it got up to the tree house, Jennifer pulled it inside. Then Tony tied the rope around the other chair and moved it up to the tree house too. "My arms aren't even tired!" he yelled happily.

1. Recognizing Words in Context

Find the word *hoist* in the passage. One definition below is closest to the meaning of that word. One definition has the opposite or nearly opposite meaning. The remaining definition has a completely different meaning. Label the definitions C for *closest*, O for *opposite or nearly opposite*, and D for *different*.

_____ a. lift

_____ b. welcome

_____ c. drop

2. Distinguishing Fact from Opinion

Two of the statements below present *facts,* which can be proved correct. The other statement is an *opinion,* which expresses someone's thoughts or beliefs. Label the statements F for *fact* and O for *opinion*.

_____ a. Dad attached the pulley to the tree house.

_____ b. Chairs don't belong in a tree house.

_____ c. They wanted chairs in the tree house.

3. Keeping Events in Order

Label the statements below 1, 2, and 3 to show the order in which the events happened.

_____ a. Tony found the beanbag chairs, and Jennifer found the rope.

_____ b. They used a pulley to lift the chairs up to the tree house.

_____ c. They decided to pull the chairs up with a rope.

4. Making Correct Inferences

Two of the statements below are correct *inferences,* or reasonable guesses. They are based on information in the passage. The other statement is an incorrect, or faulty, inference. Label the statements C for *correct* inference and F for *faulty* inference.

_____ a. A pulley can make it easier to lift something.

_____ b. Tony and Jennifer liked to play cards in their tree house.

_____ c. Tony and Jennifer did not work well together to solve the problem.

5. Understanding Main Ideas

One of the statements below expresses the main idea of the passage. One statement is too general, or too broad. The other explains only part of the passage; it is too narrow. Label the statements M for *main idea,* B for *too broad,* and N for *too narrow.*

_____ a. Tony and Jennifer used a pulley to help them solve a problem.

_____ b. Dad hung the pulley above the window.

_____ c. Tony and Jennifer had a tree house.

Correct Answers, Part A _____

Correct Answers, Part B _____

Total Correct Answers _____

The Scientific Discoveries of Benjamin Franklin

Scientists ask questions. They want to know why something happens. To find out, they watch what happens and then think of an idea that explains how and why it works. This idea is called a hypothesis. Once a scientist has a hypothesis, he or she performs an experiment to see if the hypothesis is correct.

Benjamin Franklin was a scientist. He lived in the 1700s. At that time, people did not understand what lightning was. Franklin thought that it was the same thing as electricity. It was known that electricity could make sparks. If Franklin could get lightning to make sparks, then he would prove that lightning and electricity were the same thing.

Franklin thought that he could use a kite to attract lightning from a cloud. He built his kite out of two wooden sticks and a large silk handkerchief. He put a piece of pointed metal at the top of the kite. He tied a key to the end of the kite string. When a storm was coming, he went out in a field where there was a small shed. He got the kite up and then stood in the shed. When he saw that the threads of the string were beginning to stand on end, he touched the key with his knuckle. He saw a spark. Before the rain had ended, he was able to get many more sparks.

Franklin made other important scientific discoveries. Years before he flew his kite, he had thought it possible to predict which way storms would move. To learn more about storms, he chased a whirlwind on horseback. On the basis of what he found out, Franklin made weather forecasts. He was also a printer, so he published his forecasts.

In his lifetime, Franklin sailed across the Atlantic Ocean to Europe eight times. Onboard ship, he was curious about ocean currents. On each trip, he took the temperature of the water. He used his findings to chart one of the ocean's most important currents, the Gulf Stream.

Like some other great scientists, Franklin was an inventor too. He used what he learned from science to invent things to make people's lives safer and easier. He invented the lightning rod. A lightning rod can keep buildings and ships from being damaged by lightning. He built a wood stove to heat homes. It used less wood and was safer than a fireplace.

Reading Time _____

Recalling Facts

1. A scientist's idea of how something works is called
   - ❏ a. an experiment.
   - ❏ b. a spark.
   - ❏ c. a hypothesis.

2. Benjamin Franklin lived in the
   - ❏ a. 1700s.
   - ❏ b. 1600s.
   - ❏ c. 1800s.

3. Franklin tied the end of his kite string to a
   - ❏ a. key.
   - ❏ b. lightning rod.
   - ❏ c. shed.

4. Franklin sailed to Europe
   - ❏ a. six times.
   - ❏ b. four times.
   - ❏ c. eight times.

5. Franklin invented
   - ❏ a. kites.
   - ❏ b. lightning rods.
   - ❏ c. keys.

Understanding Ideas

6. Scientists do experiments to
   - ❏ a. ask questions.
   - ❏ b. find out if a hypothesis is correct.
   - ❏ c. change the weather.

7. Benjamin Franklin proved that
   - ❏ a. lightning and electricity are different.
   - ❏ b. lightning is electricity.
   - ❏ c. kites can fly.

8. The article suggests that Franklin used a kite in his experiment because he thought a kite could
   - ❏ a. measure the distance to the clouds.
   - ❏ b. attract lightning.
   - ❏ c. show the direction of a storm.

9. You can conclude that Franklin was a great scientist because he
   - ❏ a. was an inventor.
   - ❏ b. made many important scientific discoveries.
   - ❏ c. published his own weather forecasts.

10. If you wanted to know how wood floats, you would first
   - ❏ a. think of a hypothesis.
   - ❏ b. take the temperature of the water.
   - ❏ c. do an experiment.

How Do Kites Fly?

When you watch a colorful kite fly against a blue sky, do you wonder how it stays up there? It takes wind to fly a kite. Wind has force. The surface of a kite is curved. As the wind blows across a curved surface, it causes an increase in air pressure. The surface of the kite is facing downward, and so the pressure underneath the kite is high. The pressure pushes the kite upward.

A kite cannot rise forever because of the string to which it is attached. As a person lets out more and more string, the weight of the string increases. If the weight of the string in the air gets close to the weight of the kite, the kite will start to descend.

Kites weigh very little, so it doesn't take much wind to lift them. Sometimes a kite is so light that it needs a tail to add weight and balance to keep it from tumbling and turning.

Kites come in lots of shapes, but they all have curved surfaces. A flat kite wouldn't fly because there would be no lift.

People have been flying kites for about 2,500 years. Kites were the first type of aircraft.

1. **Recognizing Words in Context**

   Find the word *descend* in the passage. One definition below is closest to the meaning of that word. One definition has the opposite or nearly opposite meaning. The remaining definition has a completely different meaning. Label the definitions C for *closest*, O for *opposite or nearly opposite*, and D for *different*.

   _____ a. fall

   _____ b. rise

   _____ c. rip

2. **Distinguishing Fact from Opinion**

   Two of the statements below present facts, which can be proved correct. The other statement is an *opinion*, which expresses someone's thoughts or beliefs. Label the statements F for *fact* and O for *opinion*.

   _____ a. Kites are fun to fly.

   _____ b. Kites weigh very little.

   _____ c. Kites have a curved surface.

3. Keeping Events in Order

Label the statements below 1, 2, and 3 to show the order in which the events happen.

_____ a. The kite flies higher.

_____ b. The kite stops rising.

_____ c. The string is let out.

4. Making Correct Inferences

Two of the statements below are correct *inferences,* or reasonable guesses. They are based on information in the passage. The other statement is an incorrect, or faulty, inference. Label the statements C for *correct* inference and F for *faulty* inference.

_____ a. A kite can fly on a windless day.

_____ b. If someone lets go of the string, the kite will rise and fly away.

_____ c. A very heavy kite would not fly.

5. Understanding Main Ideas

One of the statements below expresses the main idea of the passage. One statement is too general, or too broad. The other explains only part of the passage; it is too narrow. Label the statements M for *main idea,* B for *too broad,* and N for *too narrow.*

_____ a. Kites fly in the wind because they have a curved surface and they weigh very little.

_____ b. Sometimes a kite needs a tail.

_____ c. Kites fly in the wind.

Correct Answers, Part A _____

Correct Answers, Part B _____

Total Correct Answers _____

The Truth About Sharks

There are many myths, or false ideas, about sharks. One is that sharks like to eat people. Although some sharks can eat people, we really aren't on their menu. Sharks usually eat fish or sea mammals such as seals, especially if the fish or mammals are weak or dead.

The whale shark is Earth's biggest fish. Although whales are bigger, they are mammals, not fish. The great white shark is perhaps the most dangerous to people. Great whites are large sharks and are known to attack people. These attacks are rare. It is believed that they happen when a shark mistakes a person for something else.

Because sharks have been around since ancient times, they are thought to be primitive, simple animals. This is another myth. Sharks are really very complicated. They have a powerful sense of smell and sharp hearing. Some have organs on their snouts that pick up electric currents made by the muscles of swimming fish. Sharks have large brains, and they learn quickly. They have a memory and can be trained. Many sharks have rows of sharp teeth. When teeth are lost, other teeth move in to replace them.

Another myth about sharks is that they don't see very well. Actually, sharks have good vision, especially in dim light. They have a layer of cells at the back of the eye that works like a mirror to strengthen the light.

One myth that was created by movies is that when a shark is getting ready to attack, you can see its back fin above the water. The truth is that a shark often attacks from below, without showing its fin above the surface.

Sharks have a reputation as being dangerous, and so some people think it would be better if there were no sharks at all. This is a bad idea. Sharks are scavengers. They clean up garbage from ships and waste from the ocean. They help other species of sea animals stay strong by eating animals that are sick or weak.

Much of what we know about sharks comes from the scientists who have studied them. Dr. Eugenie Clark has made many dives to study sharks. She has also studied sharks in her lab. For example, she trained them to press a target to get food and learned how sharks can identify color and shape. Because of her work with sharks, Clark is known as the Shark Lady.

Reading Time _____

Recalling Facts

1. One myth about sharks is that they
   - ❏ a. have sharp hearing.
   - ❏ b. rarely attack humans.
   - ❏ c. like to eat humans.

2. A shark's eye
   - ❏ a. doesn't see very well.
   - ❏ b. sees well in dim light.
   - ❏ c. is like a fly's eye.

3. Some sharks have organs on their snouts that
   - ❏ a. pick up electric currents.
   - ❏ b. grow new teeth.
   - ❏ c. help them see in low light.

4. Earth's biggest fish is the
   - ❏ a. whale shark.
   - ❏ b. blue whale.
   - ❏ c. great white shark.

5. Dr. Eugenie Clark trained sharks to
   - ❏ a. clean up garbage from ships.
   - ❏ b. press a target to get food.
   - ❏ c. raise and lower their back fins.

Understanding Ideas

6. From the information in this article, you can conclude that sharks
   - ❏ a. are a threat to ships.
   - ❏ b. play a positive role in nature.
   - ❏ c. are primitive, simple animals.

7. Sharks are most likely to eat
   - ❏ a. people.
   - ❏ b. other fish.
   - ❏ c. squid.

8. Sharks can be trained because they
   - ❏ a. have sharp hearing.
   - ❏ b. are scavengers.
   - ❏ c. have a memory.

9. It is likely that Dr. Eugenie Clark
   - ❏ a. is an experienced diver.
   - ❏ b. is afraid of sharks.
   - ❏ c. does not like fish.

10. Most of the facts we know about sharks come from
    - ❏ a. the movies.
    - ❏ b. ancient times.
    - ❏ c. scientists who study sharks.

The Crittercam

One day Greg Marshall was exploring a coral reef when a shark swam by. It had a remora stuck to it. A remora is a fish that attaches itself to the skin of bigger fish to get a free ride. Marshall wished that he could observe the shark's life as well as the remora could. He had an idea. Why couldn't a camera be attached to a shark, just like a remora? This is how the Crittercam was born.

The Crittercam is shaped like a torpedo, so it slides smoothly through the water. It does not bother the shark. It is secured to the shark in a way that does not hurt its skin. The Crittercam takes videos and sends signals. These signals allow scientists in a boat to track the shark's movements. The Crittercam can record how deep and how fast the shark swims. After a while, the wire attached to the Crittercam dissolves in the salt water. Then the boat picks up the Crittercam.

Marshall used the Crittercam on white sharks for a film. The videos showed how sharks hunt. From far below the surface, sharks watch for shadows above them. Then they strike.

Before the Crittercam, a shark could be tracked only briefly. Now scientists can watch a shark's every move and see what it sees. The Crittercam can be used on other animals, both in the sea and on land.

1. **Recognizing Words in Context**

   Find the word *secured* in the passage. One definition below is closest to the meaning of that word. One definition has the opposite or nearly opposite meaning. The remaining definition has a completely different meaning. Label the definitions C for *closest,* O for *opposite or nearly opposite,* and D for *different.*

   _____ a. hidden

   _____ b. attached

   _____ c. removed

2. **Distinguishing Fact from Opinion**

   Two of the statements below present *facts,* which can be proved correct. The other statement is an *opinion,* which expresses someone's thoughts or beliefs. Label the statements F for *fact* and O for *opinion.*

   _____ a. Remoras are fish.

   _____ b. The Crittercam is shaped like a torpedo.

   _____ c. The Crittercam is a great invention.

3. Keeping Events in Order

Label the statements below 1, 2, and 3 to show the order in which the events happen.

_____ a. The Crittercam records on video.

_____ b. The boat picks up the Crittercam.

_____ c. The Crittercam floats to the surface after its wire dissolves.

4. Making Correct Inferences

Two of the statements below are correct *inferences,* or reasonable guesses. They are based on information in the passage. The other statement is an incorrect, or faulty, inference. Label the statements C for *correct* inference and F for *faulty* inference.

_____ a. The Crittercam helps scientists learn more about sharks.

_____ b. A Crittercam could also be attached to a whale.

_____ c. A shark attacks more fish when it is carrying a Crittercam.

5. Understanding Main Ideas

One of the statements below expresses the main idea of the passage. One statement is too general, or too broad. The other explains only part of the passage; it is too narrow. Label the statements M for *main idea,* B for *too broad,* and N for *too narrow.*

_____ a. The Crittercam was invented by Greg Marshall to help scientists get new information.

_____ b. Scientists have different ways of studying sharks.

_____ c. The Crittercam sends out signals to a boat.

Correct Answers, Part A _____

Correct Answers, Part B _____

Total Correct Answers _____

Types of Clouds

Have you ever watched clouds on a summer day? One cloud might look like a woolly sheep, while another one might remind you of a dog's tail. Some clouds might look like ocean waves or mountains. When you look at clouds, you will notice that there are many different kinds. Some clouds are high and thin, some are white and fluffy, and others look dark and heavy.

There are four kinds of clouds. They are high clouds, middle clouds, low clouds, and clouds that grow vertically. The clouds in these groups are named for the way they look.

Cirrus clouds are high clouds that are more than 5 kilometers (3 miles) above Earth. The air that high in the sky is very cold. Cirrus clouds are made of ice crystals that are so light that the wind blows them into thin strands. The word *cirrus* means "curl of hair." Some high clouds that look like layers or sheets are called cirrostratus clouds. The word *stratus* means "layer." There are other high clouds that look like clumps of cotton. These are the cirrocumulus clouds. *Cumulus* means "heap."

About 3 to 6.5 kilometers (2 to 4 miles) above Earth are the middle clouds. Altostratus clouds are light gray and can form a layer that looks like a blanket. Altocumulus clouds are very fluffy. They often are scattered across the sky. Another cloud that sometimes can be a middle cloud is the nimbostratus cloud. *Nimbo* comes from the word *nimbus,* which means "heavy rain." These clouds make a gray layer from which rain and snow falls. Nimbostratus clouds also can be low clouds.

The low clouds are no higher than about 1.6 kilometers (1 mile) above Earth. Two kinds of clouds are often found here. Stratocumulus clouds are light and dark and are made up of piles of fluffy clouds. Stratus clouds are very low clouds that spread out in a gray layer. They often give off moisture in the form of drizzle. Sometimes clouds form very close to the ground and become fog.

The fourth group of clouds grows vertically. These clouds have a base near the ground but rise to a great height. Cumulus clouds can pile up on top of one another. When they pile up high, they are called cumulonimbus clouds. These cloud towers can rise as high as 18 kilometers (11 miles)! Cumulonimbus clouds are also known as thunderheads because they bring thunderstorms.

Reading Time _____

Recalling Facts

1. Middle clouds are
   - ❏ a. at least 13 kilometers above Earth.
   - ❏ b. about 3 to 6.5 kilometers above Earth.
   - ❏ c. 1.6 kilometers above Earth.

2. Cirrus clouds are
   - ❏ a. high clouds.
   - ❏ b. clouds that grow vertically.
   - ❏ c. middle clouds.

3. Altostratus clouds are
   - ❏ a. clouds that grow vertically.
   - ❏ b. middle clouds.
   - ❏ c. fog.

4. Cumulonimbus clouds are also called
   - ❏ a. nimbostratus.
   - ❏ b. high clouds.
   - ❏ c. thunderheads.

5. *Cirrus* means
   - ❏ a. curl of hair.
   - ❏ b. heap.
   - ❏ c. layer.

Understanding Ideas

6. You can conclude from the article that a cirrus cloud is a
   - ❏ a. cold cloud.
   - ❏ b. low cloud.
   - ❏ c. warm cloud.

7. The article suggests that fog is
   - ❏ a. hot.
   - ❏ b. a cirrus cloud.
   - ❏ c. damp.

8. From the information, you can conclude that clouds that form heaps can be
   - ❏ a. low clouds only.
   - ❏ b. high clouds only.
   - ❏ c. high, middle, and low clouds.

9. You can conclude that clouds that grow vertically are
   - ❏ a. flat.
   - ❏ b. very tall.
   - ❏ c. low.

10. You are most likely to see a cumulonimbus cloud
    - ❏ a. just before a storm.
    - ❏ b. in a clear sky.
    - ❏ c. lying along the ground.

Meteorologists are scientists who study the weather. They also make weather forecasts. They use tools to take weather data.

One tool that measures weather is a radiosonde. This is a small box on a weather balloon. First the balloon rises. Next the box records air pressure, temperature, and humidity. Then a radio sends the data back to a base.

Another tool is Doppler radar. A radar base sends out radio waves. The waves hit rain or snow and bounce back to the base. How long it takes the waves to bounce back tells how far away the rain or snow is. Radar can also read wind speed.

Weather satellites also provide data. They orbit Earth and send back photos of clouds. There are two kinds of weather satellites. One kind moves at a speed that keeps it above the same place on Earth. Another kind passes in a much lower orbit over different parts of Earth and provides more detailed photographs.

High-speed computers compile data from all of these tools. Meteorologists put the data together to make maps and charts. They know how the weather changes. They use the data and their knowledge to make forecasts.

1. **Recognizing Words in Context**

   Find the word *compile* in the passage. One definition below is closest to the meaning of that word. One definition has the opposite or nearly opposite meaning. The remaining definition has a completely different meaning. Label the definitions C for *closest,* O for *opposite or nearly opposite,* and D for *different.*

   _____ a. scatter

   _____ b. collect

   _____ c. stack

2. **Distinguishing Fact from Opinion**

   Two of the statements below present *facts,* which can be proved correct. The other statement is an *opinion,* which expresses someone's thoughts or beliefs. Label the statements F for *fact* and O for *opinion.*

   _____ a. Weather forecasts are very helpful.

   _____ b. A radiosonde collects weather data.

   _____ c. Radar reads wind speed.

3. **Keeping Events in Order**

Label the statements below 1, 2, and 3 to show the order in which the events happen.

_____ a. A radio sends the readings back to a base.

_____ b. The balloon rises.

_____ c. The radiosonde takes readings.

4. **Making Correct Inferences**

Two of the statements below are correct *inferences,* or reasonable guesses. They are based on information in the passage. The other statement is an incorrect, or faulty, inference. Label the statements C for *correct* inference and F for *faulty* inference.

_____ a. Meteorologists can use Doppler radar to tell how fast a storm is moving.

_____ b. Weather satellites carry cameras.

_____ c. Weather balloons can be used over and over.

5. **Understanding Main Ideas**

One of the statements below expresses the main idea of the passage. One statement is too general, or too broad. The other explains only part of the passage; it is too narrow. Label the statements M for *main idea,* B for *too broad,* and N for *too narrow.*

_____ a. Meteorologists use special tools to help make weather forecasts.

_____ b. Weather satellites send back pictures of clouds.

_____ c. Meteorologists are scientists.

Correct Answers, Part A _____

Correct Answers, Part B _____

Total Correct Answers _____

Fruits and Vegetables:
A Key to Good Health

Each of us should eat five to nine servings of fruits and vegetables a day. In fact, one-third of all we eat should be fruits and vegetables. This may seem like a lot, but if you can do it your body will thank you.

Fruits and vegetables are plants. When we eat them, we get the energy that the plants get from the sun. Plants contain water, which can make us less thirsty. They have fiber, which can help remove harmful materials from our bodies. Eating raw vegetables also can help keep our teeth clean.

Plant foods are high in phytochemicals. *Phyto-* means "plant." These plant chemicals work in many ways to help us stay healthy. They fight disease and make our bodies work better. Plants that have bright colors—such as red, green, and yellow—contain the most phytochemicals. Most orange vegetables contain beta carotene, which enables our bodies to produce vitamin A. Vitamin A is needed for good eyesight and healthy skin. Vitamin C is found in large amounts in oranges, melons, and broccoli. Vitamin C helps us grow blood vessels, bones, and teeth. Why not just take vitamins in a pill? Most vitamin pills do not have as many kinds of vitamins as plants. Also, the vitamins in plants are easier for our bodies to use than the vitamins in pills are.

Unfortunately, most young people eat only one or two servings of fruits and vegetables a day. It is not difficult to add more fruits and vegetables to your diet. Put fruit on cereal for breakfast. Munch raw veggies at lunch instead of chips. A glass of real fruit juice instead of a soda is a healthful choice. Many fruits and vegetables make easy snacks. Eat a banana after school. Have a handful of grapes or an apple while doing homework. A salad with dinner and a slice of melon for dessert are other ways to get in the five to nine daily servings of fruits and vegetables.

A fruit or vegetable smoothie is a tasty dessert. You can cut up bananas, strawberries, or peaches and put them into a blender, along with a small amount of juice or milk. Frozen yogurt can be added for thickness. Both fruits and vegetables can be used to make smoothies as desserts. These can provide important nutrients while we enjoy the taste of delicious foods.

Reading Time _____

Recalling Facts

1. Every day we should eat _____ servings of fruits and vegetables.
   - ❏ a. one to four
   - ❏ b. five to nine
   - ❏ c. seven to ten

2. Phytochemicals
   - ❏ a. help fight disease.
   - ❏ b. are vitamin pills.
   - ❏ c. are found in soda.

3. Beta carotene is found in
   - ❏ a. fiber.
   - ❏ b. orange vegetables.
   - ❏ c. water.

4. Vitamin pills have
   - ❏ a. vitamins that are harder for our bodies to use than the ones in plants.
   - ❏ b. vitamins that are easier for our bodies to use than the ones in plants.
   - ❏ c. the same amounts of vitamins as plants.

5. Most young people eat _____ the amount of fruits and vegetables they need.
   - ❏ a. three times
   - ❏ b. twice
   - ❏ c. less than half

Understanding Ideas

6. To stay healthy, we should
   - ❏ a. eat lots of fruits and vegetables.
   - ❏ b. eat the food that tastes best.
   - ❏ c. avoid phytochemicals.

7. We are likely to find the most phytochemicals in
   - ❏ a. pale yellow corn.
   - ❏ b. white onions.
   - ❏ c. bright green broccoli.

8. Of the following vegetables, the one that likely has the most beta carotene is
   - ❏ a. a carrot.
   - ❏ b. lettuce.
   - ❏ c. a potato.

9. Of the following desserts, the most healthful one is
   - ❏ a. pecan pie.
   - ❏ b. fresh strawberries.
   - ❏ c. a hot-fudge sundae.

10. You can conclude from reading this article that
    - ❏ a. it is important to eat a lot of fruits and vegetables.
    - ❏ b. vegetables should be cooked before being eaten.
    - ❏ c. it is best to have fruit only for dessert.

11 B   Exotic Fruits

The word *exotic* means "from somewhere else," or "unusual." Some fruits are thought of as exotic. They include kiwifruit, mangoes, and uniq fruit.

Kiwifruit grows on vines in Asia, New Zealand, and California. This fruit is small and egg shaped, with a thin skin covered with brown fuzz. The inside of the fruit, called the flesh, is green and juicy. It has small, dark purple seeds. Before eating a kiwifruit, remove the skin. Kiwifruit provides vitamins C and E.

Mangoes come in a variety of shapes and sizes. Often they are oval and about the size of an orange. The skin can be red, green, or yellow, and the flesh is orange. Mangoes grow on evergreen trees in warm areas of the world called the tropics. Mangoes first grew in India, so they are native to that country. Mangoes have vitamins A and C and are high in fiber. Remove the peel and the pit before eating a mango.

The uniq fruit was first found in Jamaica. It came from an accidental cross between a type of orange and a grapefruit. Uniq fruits are now grown in Florida. They are sometimes called Ugli fruit because of their puffy, greenish-yellow skin. To eat one, peel it and eat it like an orange or cut it in half and eat it like a grapefruit. Like oranges, uniq fruits have lots of vitamin C.

1. **Recognizing Words in Context**

   Find the word *native* in the passage. One definition below is closest to the meaning of that word. One definition has the opposite or nearly opposite meaning. The remaining definition has a completely different meaning. Label the definitions C for *closest*, O for *opposite or nearly opposite*, and D for *different*.

   _____ a. originally from

   _____ b. from somewhere else

   _____ c. from America

2. **Distinguishing Fact from Opinion**

   Two of the statements below present *facts*, which can be proved correct. The other statement is an *opinion*, which expresses someone's thoughts or beliefs. Label the statements F for *fact* and O for *opinion*.

   _____ a. Kiwifruit grows on vines.

   _____ b. Mangoes grew first in India.

   _____ c. Mangoes taste better than uniq fruit.

3. Keeping Events in Order

Label the statements below 1, 2, and 3 to show the order in which the steps should be performed.

_____ a. Remove the pit.

_____ b. Cut off the mango's skin.

_____ c. Eat the flesh.

4. Making Correct Inferences

Two of the statements below are correct *inferences,* or reasonable guesses. They are based on information in the passage. The other statement is an incorrect, or faulty, inference. Label the statements C for *correct* inference and F for *faulty* inference.

_____ a. Kiwifruit, mangoes, and uniq fruits are all exotic fruits.

_____ b. All exotic fruits are much more expensive than other fruits.

_____ c. Some exotic fruits are healthful to eat.

5. Understanding Main Ideas

One of the statements below expresses the main idea of the passage. One statement is too general, or too broad. The other explains only part of the passage; it is too narrow. Label the statements M for *main idea,* B for *too broad,* and N for *too narrow.*

_____ a. Some fruits are exotic.

_____ b. Kiwifruit, mangoes, and uniq fruit are exotic and good for you.

_____ c. The uniq fruit was first found in Jamaica.

Correct Answers, Part A _____

Correct Answers, Part B _____

Total Correct Answers _____

Crossing the Land with Steam Power

At the end of the 18th century, land travel was slow and difficult. Most people did not travel far or very often. People might walk, ride a horse, or take a horse-drawn carriage. Farmers could not send their crops very far to market. Mail and goods took a long time to get from one place to another. Then people began to build railroads for trains powered by steam locomotives. Steam power put people and goods on the move.

A steam engine changes steam energy to mechanical energy. Mechanical energy can be used to run engines and other types of machines. The first steam engine was very simple. Water in a cylinder was heated until it boiled. Boiling water changes to steam. Steam expands. The steam pushed up a machine part called a piston. As the cylinder cooled, it created suction that pulled the piston back down.

In 1705 a steam engine was made to run a pump in England. The pump drew water out of flooded mines. Then, in 1763, James Watt built a better steam engine. He developed it into one that used pistons to turn a wheel. It could power many types of machines that used circular motion.

Other English inventors made steam engines that could power vehicles. Richard Trevithick used a high-pressure steam engine to make the first steam locomotive. It pulled 10 tons of iron and 70 men on nine miles of track. It made just one trip, but that trip showed that steam power could pull rail cars. Later, in 1825, the first true railroad was in use in England. It carried people and goods on regular runs.

The first railroad in the United States was the Baltimore and Ohio (B&O). Horses had been pulling cars on a set of tracks. The tracks had sharp curves. The B&O wanted to try steam power, but English trains were too big for the tracks. Peter Cooper built a smaller train called the *Tom Thumb*. In 1830, the *Tom Thumb* made its first run. Ten years later, there were more than 2,000 miles of track in our country.

The railroads grew rapidly. By 1869 they ran all the way from the East Coast to the West Coast. People, goods, and mail moved quickly and safely. Steam power took them over the rails and across the land. Trips that once took weeks now took just two or three days.

Reading Time _____

Recalling Facts

1. At the end of the 18th century, land travel was
   - ❏ a. by train.
   - ❏ b. slow and difficult.
   - ❏ c. fast and easy.

2. Steam engines change steam energy to
   - ❏ a. heat.
   - ❏ b. mechanical energy.
   - ❏ c. boiling water.

3. James Watt built an engine that could
   - ❏ a. turn a wheel.
   - ❏ b. change suction to steam energy.
   - ❏ c. power a car.

4. Richard Trevithick built the
   - ❏ a. B&O.
   - ❏ b. *Tom Thumb*.
   - ❏ c. first steam locomotive.

5. Railroads ran from coast to coast in the United States by
   - ❏ a. 1869.
   - ❏ b. 1705.
   - ❏ c. 1825.

Understanding Ideas

6. From reading the article, you can conclude that English inventors
   - ❏ a. were smarter than all other inventors.
   - ❏ b. developed the steam engine.
   - ❏ c. discovered steam.

7. You can conclude from the article that steam locomotives
   - ❏ a. were slow.
   - ❏ b. could pull very heavy loads.
   - ❏ c. could do more work than 50 horses.

8. The B&O needed a smaller locomotive because
   - ❏ a. it could go all the way from coast to coast.
   - ❏ b. the curves in the B&O's track were too sharp for the big English locomotives.
   - ❏ c. horses could pull it more easily.

9. Factories produced more goods after the steam engine was invented because
   - ❏ a. more factory workers could ride trains to their jobs.
   - ❏ b. coal mines produced more coal.
   - ❏ c. the factories began using machines powered by steam engines.

10. You can conclude that railroads grew quickly in the United States because they
    - ❏ a. were needed to move people and goods long distances.
    - ❏ b. cost less to ride than horse-drawn carriages.
    - ❏ c. ran on tracks.

Robert Fulton and the Steamboat

In the early 1700s, people had dreams of using steam to run boats. But they were just dreams. The first steam engines did not have enough power to run a boat. After James Watt built a better steam engine in 1763, the way was open for the dreams to become real.

A few inventors built early steamboats. In 1786, John Fitch built the first one in the United States. The boat had a steam engine that moved rows of oars through the water. It often broke down, however, and people did not take it very seriously.

Robert Fulton made the steamboat popular. Fulton was an American who went to London to study art. While he was there, he became intrigued by the study of mechanics. First he came up with a new kind of canal system and then a small steamboat. It traveled up the Seine River in France at 5 kilometers (3 miles) per hour.

Four years later, Fulton came back to the United States. President Jefferson wanted him to build canals, but Fulton wanted to build a new steamboat. His new boat had a flat bottom. There were paddle wheels on each side. People called it Fulton's Folly. The boat's real name was the *Clermont*. In 1807, the *Clermont* went from New York City to Albany in just 32 hours. The same trip took an average of four days by sailboat. Soon steamboats were in use on many rivers.

1. Recognizing Words in Context

Find the word *intrigued* in the passage. One definition below is closest to the meaning of that word. One definition has the opposite or nearly opposite meaning. The remaining definition has a completely different meaning. Label the definitions C for *closest,* O for *opposite or nearly opposite,* and D for *different.*

_____ a. invented

_____ b. interested

_____ c. bored

2. Distinguishing Fact from Opinion

Two of the statements below present *facts,* which can be proved correct. The other statement is an *opinion,* which expresses someone's thoughts or beliefs. Label the statements F for *fact* and O for *opinion.*

_____ a. James Watt built a better steam engine in 1763.

_____ b. The *Clermont* had paddle wheels.

_____ c. Steamboats are better than sailboats.

3. Keeping Events in Order

Label the statements below 1, 2, and 3 to show the order in which the events happened.

_____ a. Fulton designed canals.

_____ b. Fulton built the *Clermont*.

_____ c. Fulton went to London to study art.

4. Making Correct Inferences

Two of the statements below are correct *inferences,* or reasonable guesses. They are based on information in the passage. The other statement is an incorrect, or faulty, inference. Label the statements C for *correct* inference and F for *faulty* inference.

_____ a. Steamboats were faster than sailboats.

_____ b. Fulton liked living in London better than in the United States.

_____ c. Robert Fulton was an inventor.

5. Understanding Main Ideas

One of the statements below expresses the main idea of the passage. One statement is too general, or too broad. The other explains only part of the passage; it is too narrow. Label the statements M for *main idea,* B for *too broad,* and N for *too narrow.*

_____ a. The *Clermont* went from New York to Albany in 32 hours.

_____ b. Robert Fulton was responsible for the first successful steamboat service.

_____ c. Steam engines were used to run boats and trains.

Correct Answers, Part A _____

Correct Answers, Part B _____

Total Correct Answers _____

Seasons Around the World

The seasons of the year are spring, summer, fall, and winter. They bring changes in temperature and weather. They also bring changes in the lengths of days. On summer days there are more hours of daylight than on winter days.

There are two reasons that the seasons and the hours of daylight change. The first is that Earth moves around the Sun, and the second is that the axis of Earth is tilted. Imagine Earth as a big ball with a line going through its middle. At the top of the line is the North Pole. At the bottom is the South Pole. The line is Earth's axis, on which it turns. Now imagine that the line is not straight up and down, but tilted.

Picture the tilted Earth as it moves around the Sun. Sometimes Earth's top half, which is called the Northern Hemisphere, is tilted toward the Sun. At the same time, the bottom half, or Southern Hemisphere, is tilted away from the Sun. At other times, the Southern Hemisphere is tilted toward the Sun, and the Northern Hemisphere is tilted away.

The half of Earth that is tilted toward the Sun gets more of the Sun's light and heat. In this part of the world, it is summer. The half that is tilted away from the Sun gets less sunlight and heat. In this part of the world, it is winter. When it is summer in the United States, it is winter in Australia. The United States is in the Northern Hemisphere, and Australia is in the Southern Hemisphere.

The equator stays the same distance from the Sun all the time. The temperature stays the same, and the hours of daylight do not change. Therefore, there are no seasons. However, the amount of rain does change. Places on the equator have a wet season and a dry season.

What happens at the North and South Poles? The Sun shines all day at the start of summer. It is dark all day at the start of winter.

Once a year, the Sun reaches its most northern point in the sky. This happens in June, and in the Northern Hemisphere it is called the summer solstice. This is the day with the most hours of daylight. In December, the Sun reaches its most southern point. This is our winter solstice, the day with the fewest hours of daylight.

Reading Time _____

Recalling Facts

1. The reasons the seasons change are
   - ❏ a. the North Pole is at the top of Earth, and the South Pole is at the bottom.
   - ❏ b. Earth moves around the Sun, and Earth's axis is tilted.
   - ❏ c. the Northern Hemisphere is tilted toward the Sun, and the Sun gives off energy.

2. Places near the equator have
   - ❏ a. spring, summer, winter, and fall.
   - ❏ b. a wet season and a dry season.
   - ❏ c. a light season and a dark season.

3. When the Sun is at its most northern point, it is
   - ❏ a. fall.
   - ❏ b. December.
   - ❏ c. June.

4. In the Southern Hemisphere, it is winter in
   - ❏ a. June.
   - ❏ b. December.
   - ❏ c. January.

5. Australia is located
   - ❏ a. in the Northern Hemisphere.
   - ❏ b. in the Southern Hemisphere.
   - ❏ c. on the equator.

Understanding Ideas

6. When the Northern Hemisphere is tilted toward the Sun, the Southern Hemisphere is tilted away from the Sun because the
   - ❏ a. Earth rotates on its axis.
   - ❏ b. Earth's axis is tilted.
   - ❏ c. winter is colder than summer.

7. When the Northern Hemisphere is most tilted toward the Sun, it is
   - ❏ a. summer in New Jersey.
   - ❏ b. winter in New Jersey.
   - ❏ c. summer in Australia.

8. When it is winter at the North Pole, it is _____ at the South Pole.
   - ❏ a. summer
   - ❏ b. winter
   - ❏ c. spring

9. At the North and South Poles, the Sun
   - ❏ a. never shines.
   - ❏ b. never shines at the start of winter.
   - ❏ c. never shines at the start of summer.

10. In the Northern Hemisphere it is light outside longer on the
    - ❏ a. winter solstice.
    - ❏ b. first day of spring.
    - ❏ c. summer solstice.

Throughout history, people have found ways to keep warm during winter. Today we have both old ways and new ways of staying warm.

Down consists of the fine, soft feathers of a bird, such as a goose. The feathers trap air and slow down heat loss. Down has been used for hundreds of years in bed covers called comforters. Some people still like down comforters, coats, and jackets. Today, however, there is another choice. Synthetic down is made of manufactured fibers that work as well as feathers when dry and better than feathers when wet. The fibers are used in comforters and outdoor clothes.

Polar fleece is a new fabric made from recycled soda bottles. It is lightweight and warm. It keeps people dry by letting moisture pass through it and away from their bodies. Polar fleece is used for coats, jackets, hats, and gloves.

For cold fingers and toes, there are warmers that slip inside mittens or boots. These come sealed in a package. When the package is opened, the ingredients inside the warmers react to the air by heating up. Electric socks and mittens can also keep people warm. They have batteries that warm wires that run through the fabric.

1. **Recognizing Words in Context**

   Find the word *synthetic* in the passage. One definition below is closest to the meaning of that word. One definition has the opposite or nearly opposite meaning. The remaining definition has a completely different meaning. Label the definitions C for *closest,* O for *opposite or nearly opposite,* and D for *different.*

   _____ a. made by people

   _____ b. natural

   _____ c. warm

2. **Distinguishing Fact from Opinion**

   Two of the statements below present *facts,* which can be proved correct. The other statement is an *opinion,* which expresses someone's thoughts or beliefs. Label the statements F for *fact* and O for *opinion.*

   _____ a. Down is made up of fine, soft feathers.

   _____ b. Down coats are warmer than other coats.

   _____ c. Polar fleece is lightweight.

3. Keeping Events in Order

Two of the statements below describe events that happen at the same time. The other statement describes an event that happens before or after those events. Label them S for *same time*, B for *before*, and A for *after*.

_____ a. You open the package of warmers.

_____ b. The warmers react to the air by heating up.

_____ c. You expose them to air.

4. Making Correct Inferences

Two of the statements below are correct *inferences*, or reasonable guesses. They are based on information in the passage. The other statement is an incorrect, or faulty, inference. Label the statements C for *correct* inference and F for *faulty* inference.

_____ a. All down is synthetic.

_____ b. Today, there are new ways to keep warm in winter.

_____ c. A polar fleece jacket would be a good choice to wear on a cold day.

5. Understanding Main Ideas

One of the statements below expresses the main idea of the passage. One statement is too general, or too broad. The other explains only part of the passage; it is too narrow. Label the statements M for *main idea*, B for *too broad*, and N for *too narrow*.

_____ a. There is clothing for every season of the year.

_____ b. There are new ways to keep warm in winter.

_____ c. Electric socks have batteries.

Correct Answers, Part A _____

Correct Answers, Part B _____

Total Correct Answers _____

What Is a Mammal?

Mammals are warm-blooded animals that produce milk to feed their young. Female mammals have mammary glands, which produce the milk. All mammals have backbones and hair. There are about 4,600 living species of mammals. The largest mammal is the blue whale. Blue whales can grow to be more than 33 meters (100 feet) long. Shrews and mice are the smallest mammals. Some are less than 5 centimeters (2 inches) long.

Mammals live almost everywhere on Earth, including deserts, forests, grasslands, and mountains. Humans, rats, camels, skunks, lions, deer, and wolves all are mammals. You may have other mammals in your home. Dogs, cats, and hamsters are mammals.

Almost all mammals give birth to live young, but a few lay eggs. These mammals are called monotremes. Even though monotremes lay eggs, they still produce milk to feed their newly hatched young. There are only three kinds of monotremes. They are the platypus and two kinds of spiny anteaters.

Most mammals give birth to young that can live outside the mother's body right away. A few mammals have young that are born less mature. These mammals are called marsupials. Most marsupials live the first part of their lives in a pouch on their mother's body. Two kinds of marsupials are kangaroos and opossums.

Some mammals live in the water. These are called aquatic mammals, or sea mammals. Some people think that dolphins and whales are fish. They are not. They are sea mammals. Sea mammals have lungs for breathing. They must surface about every two minutes to breathe. Whales and dolphins breathe through a blowhole in the top of their heads. Some people think that whales and dolphins have no hair, but actually they do have a few hairs on their heads.

Another kind of sea mammal is the manatee, often called the sea cow. Manatees breathe through snouts that they lift above the surface of the water. Seals and walruses are also sea mammals. So are polar bears. Polar bears spend a lot of time in the water hunting for food, such as seals and fish.

About one-fourth of mammal species are threatened. So few of these animals are left that they are in danger of dying out. Some of these species' habitats have been taken over by people. Some species have been poisoned by air and water pollution. Many have been hunted for food or for skins. Several groups are working to save these species.

Reading Time _____

Recalling Facts

1. Mammals
   - ❑ a. are warm blooded.
   - ❑ b. have no backbone.
   - ❑ c. are hairless.

2. Most mammals
   - ❑ a. lay eggs.
   - ❑ b. give birth to live young.
   - ❑ c. have a pouch.

3. Mammals that lay eggs are called
   - ❑ a. monotremes.
   - ❑ b. marsupials.
   - ❑ c. shrews.

4. Whales and dolphins
   - ❑ a. lay eggs.
   - ❑ b. are fish.
   - ❑ c. breathe through a blowhole.

5. The largest mammal is the
   - ❑ a. kangaroo.
   - ❑ b. elephant.
   - ❑ c. blue whale.

Understanding Ideas

6. You can conclude from the article that mammals live
   - ❑ a. only on land.
   - ❑ b. only in water.
   - ❑ c. in most parts of the world.

7. From reading the article, you can conclude that you are a
   - ❑ a. marsupial.
   - ❑ b. mammal.
   - ❑ c. monotreme.

8. Newborn marsupials live in their mothers' pouches because they are
   - ❑ a. a threatened species.
   - ❑ b. not fully developed at birth.
   - ❑ c. afraid of being eaten.

9. Opossums are marsupials because
   - ❑ a. they lay eggs.
   - ❑ b. their newborns are underdeveloped.
   - ❑ c. their young feed on milk.

10. You can use information from the article to figure out that polar bears
   - ❑ a. can swim.
   - ❑ b. are a threatened species.
   - ❑ c. are the largest mammals.

Mammals with Pouches

Marsupials are one kind of mammal. Their young are born before they are fully formed. Most marsupials have a pouch where the young stay while they develop. While they grow in the pouch, the newborns feed on milk from the mother. When they are big enough, they leave the pouch to live on their own. Some marsupials don't have a pouch. After birth, the young attach themselves to the mother. They stay attached until they can find food on their own.

Two well-known marsupials are kangaroos and koalas. Their young are called joeys. Kangaroos have pouches in front. A kangaroo joey may stay in the pouch for as long as six months. Koalas look like small bears, and they climb trees. A koala's pouch is on its back. A koala joey also may stay in the pouch for up to six months. It might ride on its mother's back for six more months.

There are many other kinds of marsupials. Some, such as marsupial mice, are very small. Others, such as wombats, are larger. Wombats are short animals with thick fur. A wombat can be 1 meter (3¼ feet) long and weigh 16 kilograms (35 pounds). Wombats live in the ground in burrows. They eat roots and grass. They are nocturnal; that is, they sleep during the day. Tasmanian devils weigh about 9 kilograms (20 pounds) and have long tails and pointed snouts. They eat dead animals. They also hunt and kill small animals for food.

1. **Recognizing Words in Context**

   Find the word *nocturnal* in the passage. One definition below is closest to the meaning of that word. One definition has the opposite or nearly opposite meaning. The remaining definition has a completely different meaning. Label the definitions C for *closest,* O for *opposite or nearly opposite,* and D for *different.*

   _____ a. feeding on small animals

   _____ b. active during the day

   _____ c. active at night

2. **Distinguishing Fact from Opinion**

   Two of the statements below present *facts,* which can be proved correct. The other statement is an *opinion,* which expresses someone's thoughts or beliefs. Label the statements F for *fact* and O for *opinion.*

   _____ a. Kangaroos and koalas are marsupials.

   _____ b. Female kangaroos have pouches.

   _____ c. Tasmanian devils are odd looking.

3. Keeping Events in Order

Label the statements below 1, 2, and 3 to show the order in which the events happen.

_____ a. A joey is born.

_____ b. The joey leaves the pouch.

_____ c. The joey feeds on milk from its mother.

4. Making Correct Inferences

Two of the statements below are correct *inferences,* or reasonable guesses. They are based on information in the passage. The other statement is an incorrect, or faulty, inference. Label the statements C for *correct* inference and F for *faulty* inference.

_____ a. Female marsupial mice have pouches.

_____ b. Wombats are good diggers.

_____ c. Almost all marsupials sleep during the day.

5. Understanding Main Ideas

One of the statements below expresses the main idea of the passage. One statement is too general, or too broad. The other explains only part of the passage; it is too narrow. Label the statements M for *main idea,* B for *too broad,* and N for *too narrow.*

_____ a. Marsupials are born before they are fully formed.

_____ b. Mammals give birth to their young in different ways.

_____ c. A koala's pouch is on its back.

Correct Answers, Part A _____

Correct Answers, Part B _____

Total Correct Answers _____

How to Organize a Great Science Fair Project

How can you create a great science fair project? You can start by asking yourself the following questions.

(1) What interests me? You can connect almost any topic to science. Your topic could be plants, worms, dogs, the sky, or something else. If you can't think of a topic, look in books or on the Internet. Ask a librarian or your teacher for help. Your parents may have some good ideas.

(2) What question do I have about this topic? A great science project always includes an experiment. Make sure that your question can be answered by doing an experiment. Here are some examples of questions. Does the amount of light have an effect on how fast plants grow? How much salt is in different kinds of cookies sold at the store? Why does the sky change color at different times of the day?

(3)How much time do I have before the science fair? If the science fair is in two weeks, you won't have time for some types of experiments, such as growing plants. Carefully plan your project so that you have enough time to do your experiment accurately.

(4) What do I think is the answer to my question? Why do I think this? This is your hypothesis, or explanation. You will prove it right or wrong by doing an experiment. Let's look at the sky question. Your hypothesis might be "The color of the sky is related to the position of the sun."

(5) How can I prove my hypothesis? This is where the experiment comes in. You have to test your hypothesis. If you were trying to find out about how light affects plant growth, you could plant seeds in a number of containers. Then you could expose them to different amounts of light.

(6) How can I record my experiment? For the plant experiment, you might measure each plant once a week and write the data on a chart. You could take pictures of the plants each week.

(7) How can I present my results? You might use poster board to show your question and hypothesis. You might add pictures and graphs. A great science project also states a conclusion. This might be "The plants that got the most light grew the fastest."

When you are done with your project, you may have more questions. A great science project makes you want to learn even more.

Reading Time _____

Recalling Facts

1. One way to get an idea for a topic is to
   - ❏ a. ask yourself what interests you.
   - ❏ b. do an experiment.
   - ❏ c. make a display with poster board.

2. A hypothesis is
   - ❏ a. an experiment.
   - ❏ b. a question.
   - ❏ c. an explanation.

3. A great science project always includes
   - ❏ a. an experiment.
   - ❏ b. plants.
   - ❏ c. a number of containers.

4. One way to test a theory is to
   - ❏ a. draw a conclusion.
   - ❏ b. make a hypothesis.
   - ❏ c. do an experiment.

5. A great science project
   - ❏ a. makes you want to learn even more.
   - ❏ b. answers all of your science questions.
   - ❏ c. answers no questions.

Understanding Ideas

6. You can conclude from reading the article that
   - ❏ a. all science projects take about the same amount of time.
   - ❏ b. some science projects take longer than others.
   - ❏ c. all science projects take about two weeks.

7. An experiment is a very important part of a science project because
   - ❏ a. you can use it to test your hypothesis.
   - ❏ b. it can help you find a topic.
   - ❏ c. it can help you think of a question.

8. If you wanted to find out if cold water freezes faster than hot water, you would first
   - ❏ a. think of an experiment that would give you the answer.
   - ❏ b. state your conclusion.
   - ❏ c. make a chart.

9. Doing experiments can help
   - ❏ a. plants grow.
   - ❏ b. you understand how things work.
   - ❏ c. you form a hypothesis.

10. From the information in the article, you can conclude that
   - ❏ a. there are several steps to organizing a great science project.
   - ❏ b. all science projects should involve plants.
   - ❏ c. a great science project starts with a conclusion.

A Tasteful Science Experiment

Where on our tongues do we taste bitter, sweet, salty, and sour flavors? Here's an experiment to find the answer. You will need sugar, lemon juice, salt, instant coffee, a cookie sheet, and a small bowl.

On the cookie sheet, make tiny piles of sugar, salt, and coffee grains. Next, pour a few drops of lemon juice into the bowl. Then, wet your finger, dip it in the sugar and hold it against the center of your tongue. What do you taste? Now press the sugar on the front of your tongue and see if the taste varies.

Next, rinse out your mouth with water. Dip your finger into the salt and press it against the center of your tongue. Then press it on your tongue near one side and see how it tastes different.

Now rinse your mouth and try the coffee on the center of your tongue. Then try it on the back of your tongue. Rinse your mouth again. Finally, try the lemon juice in the center of your tongue, and then near the side of your tongue.

What did you learn? The center of your tongue does not taste things very well. The front of your tongue tastes sweet things, and the sides taste salty and sour things. The back of the tongue tastes bitter things.

1. **Recognizing Words in Context**

   Find the word *varies* in the passage. One definition below is closest to the meaning of that word. One definition has the opposite or nearly opposite meaning. The remaining definition has a completely different meaning. Label the definitions C for *closest*, O for *opposite or nearly opposite*, and D for *different*.

   _____ a. changes

   _____ b. weakens

   _____ c. stays the same

2. **Distinguishing Fact from Opinion**

   Two of the statements below present facts, which can be proved correct. The other statement is an *opinion*, which expresses someone's thoughts or beliefs. Label the statements F for *fact* and O for *opinion*.

   _____ a. Sour things taste worse than bitter things.

   _____ b. The center of your tongue does not taste things very well.

   _____ c. You can taste sugar at the front of your tongue.

3. **Keeping Events in Order**

   Label the statements below 1, 2, and 3 to show the order in which the steps should be performed.

   _____ a. Hold the sugar against the center of your tongue.

   _____ b. On the cookie sheet, make tiny piles of sugar, salt, and coffee grains.

   _____ c. Pour a few drops of lemon juice into the bowl.

4. **Making Correct Inferences**

   Two of the statements below are correct *inferences,* or reasonable guesses. They are based on information in the passage. The other statement is an incorrect, or faulty, inference. Label the statements C for *correct* inference and F for *faulty* inference.

   _____ a. You can taste candy well on the front of your tongue.

   _____ b. You can taste ice cream well on the center of your tongue.

   _____ c. There are different taste centers on the tongue.

5. **Understanding Main Ideas**

   One of the statements below expresses the main idea of the passage. One statement is too general, or too broad. The other explains only part of the passage; it is too narrow. Label the statements M for *main idea,* B for *too broad,* and N for *too narrow.*

   _____ a. Different parts of the tongue taste things differently.

   _____ b. You can taste sweet things on the front of your tongue.

   _____ c. The primary job of the tongue is to taste things.

Correct Answers, Part A _____

Correct Answers, Part B _____

Total Correct Answers _____

Rocks and Minerals

If you hold a rock in your hands, you are holding a piece of our planet. Earth is basically made of rock. Rock is a mass of mineral deposits. All things in nature that are not animals or plants are minerals. Some minerals, such as salt, coal, and gold, are solid. Other minerals, such as water and natural gas, are not solid.

A geologist is a scientist who studies what Earth is made of and how it was formed. Geologists classify rocks in groups. The names of the groups indicate how the rock was made. Igneous rock is formed as hot magma cools. *Igneous* means "fire-formed." Magma is melted rock that comes from deep within Earth, where the temperature is extremely high. Magma can harden and form rock if it rises to the surface of Earth. Granite is formed this way. When magma rises to the surface in a volcano, it is called lava. Rocks formed from lava are called basalts. These are the most common kinds of igneous rocks.

Sedimentary rock forms when layers of hard minerals blend together. This can happen over time or from the force of water or wind. Two common kinds of sedimentary rocks are sandstone and limestone. If you look closely at these rocks, you can see the layers.

When igneous or sedimentary rock is subjected to strong heat and pressure, it may turn into metamorphic rock. Metamorphic rock is made up of rock that has changed its form. One example is marble, which has many colors and is harder than the rocks from which it is made.

Geologists also separate rocks into groups based on how the rocks look. They call some minerals crystals. Diamonds are crystals that are made from a mineral called carbon. They are the hardest things on Earth. Graphite is pure carbon, too, but it is very soft. Graphite is used to make pencil lead. The difference in hardness is due to the amount of heat and pressure put on the carbon. Graphite is not the only soft mineral. Another is talc, which is ground up to make talcum powder.

Geologists refer to some minerals as metals. Iron is a metal. Most of the iron we use comes from the mineral hematite. This rock is red, or black with red streaks. The streaks are the iron. They are red because iron rusts when it is exposed to air and water.

Reading Time _____

Recalling Facts

1. Earth is basically made of
   - ❏ a. water.
   - ❏ b. rock.
   - ❏ c. sandstone.

2. Geologists classify rocks mainly according to
   - ❏ a. the way the rocks were formed.
   - ❏ b. where they are found.
   - ❏ c. color.

3. *Igneous* means
   - ❏ a. layered.
   - ❏ b. changed.
   - ❏ c. fire-formed.

4. Sandstone is
   - ❏ a. igneous rock.
   - ❏ b. metamorphic rock.
   - ❏ c. sedimentary rock.

5. Diamonds are formed from
   - ❏ a. hematite.
   - ❏ b. carbon.
   - ❏ c. magma.

Understanding Ideas

6. One example of a mineral is
   - ❏ a. a flea.
   - ❏ b. a fern.
   - ❏ c. water.

7. A geologist would agree that all rocks are
   - ❏ a. formed in layers.
   - ❏ b. made of minerals.
   - ❏ c. formed by volcanoes.

8. From the facts in this article, you can conclude that
   - ❏ a. diamonds are harder than marble.
   - ❏ b. granite is harder than diamonds.
   - ❏ c. sandstone is harder than diamonds.

9. If an earthquake put strong pressure on a layer of sedimentary rock, the rock might turn into
   - ❏ a. igneous rock.
   - ❏ b. iron.
   - ❏ c. metamorphic rock.

10. From reading this article, you can conclude that minerals are
   - ❏ a. always metals.
   - ❏ b. all around us.
   - ❏ c. found only in rocks.

The Hope diamond is a rare and famous gem. It has a complex history. In the 1600s, a French traveler bought a blue diamond the size of a fist. It most likely came from India. He sold the stone to the French king in 1668. The stone was recut and worn on a ribbon. When a diamond is recut, a jeweler cuts off pieces to make it shinier and give it a different shape. The recut diamond was named the French Blue. During the French Revolution, it vanished and no one knew who had it.

In 1812 it was reported that a London diamond seller had a large blue diamond. Many experts believe that it was the French Blue and that it had been recut. Later, King George IV of England owned the diamond. It was sold after he died.

By 1839 the stone belonged to Henry Philip Hope, a London banker. While Hope had the gem, it was named the Hope diamond. After Hope died, members of his family sold it to pay debts.

The next owner took it to Paris. It was sold and then resold to Pierre Cartier, a famous jeweler. He sold it to Evalyn Walsh McLean, a wealthy woman in Washington, D.C. She later had it set in a necklace. After she died, a jeweler named Harry Winston bought the diamond. Years later, he gave it to the Smithsonian Institution in Washington, D.C. It is there now for all to see.

1. **Recognizing Words in Context**

Find the word *complex* in the passage. One definition below is closest to the meaning of that word. One definition has the opposite or nearly opposite meaning. The remaining definition has a completely different meaning. Label the definitions C for *closest,* O for *opposite or nearly opposite,* and D for *different.*

_____ a. shining brightly

_____ b. simple

_____ c. having many details

2. **Distinguishing Fact from Opinion**

Two of the statements below present *facts,* which can be proved correct. The other statement is an *opinion,* which expresses someone's thoughts or beliefs. Label the statements F for *fact* and O for *opinion.*

_____ a. A museum is a good place for the Hope diamond.

_____ b. French kings owned a large blue diamond.

_____ c. The Hope diamond is now in the Smithsonian Institution.

3. Keeping Events in Order

Label the statements below 1, 2, and 3 to show the order in which the events happened.

_____ a. Henry Philip Hope bought the diamond.

_____ b. The diamond was named the Hope diamond.

_____ c. Members of Hope's family sold the diamond.

4. Making Correct Inferences

Two of the statements below are correct *inferences,* or reasonable guesses. They are based on information in the passage. The other statement is an incorrect, or faulty, inference. Label the statements C for *correct* inference and F for *faulty* inference.

_____ a. The Hope diamond has had many different owners.

_____ b. The Hope diamond was first discovered more than 300 years ago.

_____ c. Henry Philip Hope discovered the Hope diamond.

5. Understanding Main Ideas

One of the statements below expresses the main idea of the passage. One statement is too general, or too broad. The other explains only part of the passage; it is too narrow. Label the statements M for *main idea,* B for *too broad,* and N for *too narrow.*

_____ a. King George IV owned the diamond.

_____ b. The Hope diamond is famous.

_____ c. The Hope diamond has a long and fascinating history.

Correct Answers, Part A _____

Correct Answers, Part B _____

Total Correct Answers _____

Water Is Needed for Life

What would happen to a houseplant if nobody ever watered it? It would wilt and die. Animals and people need water too. In fact, all living things need water to survive.

Why is water so important? It makes up most of the weight of living things. An animal's blood and the sap of plants are mostly water. Blood and sap move food and get rid of waste. In the cells, chemical reactions take place. These are needed for survival, and they can't occur without water.

Our bodies lose water in many ways. We lose it through our skin when we sweat. We lose tiny drops of it in the air that we exhale. We lose it in the form of urine. We lose between 2 and 3 liters (2.1 to 3.2 quarts) of water a day. In order to keep enough water in our bodies for our cells to function, we need to take in enough water to make up for what is lost. We get some water from food, but we get most of it by drinking. This is why people need to drink a glass of water several times a day. On hot days, we sweat more, so we need to drink more. When the amount of water in the body falls below a certain level, we feel thirsty. Thirst is the body's way of making sure we drink what we need.

Think about the many other ways we use water each day. We use it to help us brush our teeth. We might use water to make soup for lunch. We add water to cake mixes. We give water to pets. We water the grass and the flowers in the yard. If there isn't enough rain, farmers may need to water their crops. We take a bath or shower to get clean. We use water to wash our clothes, wash the car, and mop the floor. We use water to put out fires.

Pure water does not have any taste or odor. But chemicals, pesticides, and wastes from factories have polluted our water. Water pollution can cause health problems in people and can poison wildlife. The water that we get from faucets and water fountains is specially cleaned to make it safe to drink. Laws have been passed to stop pollution. We need to do more to make sure that there will always be clean water for all of Earth's living things.

Reading Time _____

Recalling Facts

1. Water makes up _____ of the weight of living things.
   - ❏ a. a small part
   - ❏ b. almost all
   - ❏ c. most

2. We lose between _____ of water a day.
   - ❏ a. 2 and 3 pints
   - ❏ b. 2 and 3 liters
   - ❏ c. 4 and 5 liters

3. When the amount of water in our bodies falls below a certain level, we
   - ❏ a. feel thirsty.
   - ❏ b. sweat more.
   - ❏ c. take a bath or shower.

4. Blood and sap
   - ❏ a. move food and get rid of waste.
   - ❏ b. make up 90 percent of the weight of living things.
   - ❏ c. contain very little water.

5. Water pollution can be caused by
   - ❏ a. steam.
   - ❏ b. pesticides.
   - ❏ c. faucets.

Understanding Ideas

6. If there were no water on Earth, there would be no
   - ❏ a. mice.
   - ❏ b. rocks.
   - ❏ c. deserts.

7. You would probably be thirstiest after
   - ❏ a. reading a book at the library.
   - ❏ b. watching TV.
   - ❏ c. playing basketball outside on a hot day.

8. During dry weather, a farmer would think it is most important to
   - ❏ a. water the vegetable crops.
   - ❏ b. wash the tractor.
   - ❏ c. use a hose to clean the sides of the barn.

9. You might think water is polluted if it
   - ❏ a. smells bad.
   - ❏ b. has no odor.
   - ❏ c. has no taste.

10. Without water,
    - ❏ a. most animals could survive.
    - ❏ b. most plants could survive.
    - ❏ c. no living things could survive.

17 B How Cacti Survive with Little Water

Deserts are very dry places because they get so little rain. Yet plants do grow there. The cactus is one plant that has adapted to life with very little water. These plants have thick stems that can store large amounts of water. Some cacti have very tall stems. Others have stems that are round and shaped almost like a barrel.

The skin of the cactus has a waxy coating. This helps the plant hold in moisture. The stems of tall cacti have ribs that run from the top to the bottom. While the cacti are holding a lot of water, the stem is swollen and the ribs flatten out. As the stem loses water and shrinks, the ribs stand out more and more. Then the ribs help shade the stem and hold it up during the times that it is smaller. When the stem loses much of its water, it may bend. This shades part of the plant and helps keep it from losing more water.

Cacti have very small leaves or no leaves at all. They do have spines. These help shade the stem and can direct rainwater down to the roots. Cactus roots are near the surface. They spread out over a wide area. This allows them to absorb more water from rainfall. For this reason, cacti are spaced far apart.

1. **Recognizing Words in Context**

Find the word *adapted* in the passage. One definition below is closest to the meaning of that word. One definition has the opposite or nearly opposite meaning. The remaining definition has a completely different meaning. Label the definitions C for *closest*, O for *opposite or nearly opposite*, and D for *different*.

_____ a. added

_____ b. changed

_____ c. resisted

2. **Distinguishing Fact from Opinion**

Two of the statements below present *facts*, which can be proved correct. The other statement is an *opinion*, which expresses someone's thoughts or beliefs. Label the statements F for *fact* and O for *opinion*.

_____ a. Cacti have thick stems.

_____ b. Cactus roots are near the surface of the ground.

_____ c. Cactus plants are hard to grow.

3. Keeping Events in Order

Label the statements below 1, 2, and 3 to show the order in which the events happen.

_____ a. Part of the stem is protected by shade.

_____ b. The stem bends over.

_____ c. The stem begins to lose water.

4. Making Correct Inferences

Two of the statements below are correct *inferences,* or reasonable guesses. They are based on information in the passage. The other statement is an incorrect, or faulty, inference. Label the statements C for *correct* inference and F for *faulty* inference.

_____ a. The cactus has many ways of adapting to life in the desert.

_____ b. Cactus stems swell and shrink, depending on how much water they are holding.

_____ c. It never rains in the desert.

5. Understanding Main Ideas

One of the statements below expresses the main idea of the passage. One statement is too general, or too broad. The other explains only part of the passage; it is too narrow. Label the statements M for *main idea,* B for *too broad,* and N for *too narrow.*

_____ a. The skin of a cactus has a waxy coating.

_____ b. Some plants are able to live in difficult environments.

_____ c. Cactus plants are well suited to life in the desert.

Correct Answers, Part A _____

Correct Answers, Part B _____

Total Correct Answers _____

People grow flowers in order to enjoy their beauty. Flowers are nice to look at, but they have another purpose. Flowers make seeds that can grow into new plants. Plants that have flowers are called angiosperms.

A flower has four parts that are arranged around a center. The outer part is a circle made up of sepals. These are usually green and look like a ring of leaves. Sometimes they form a cup. The next part of a flower is a circle made of petals. They are larger than the sepals. Petals are the part of the flower you notice first. This is because they are usually white or a bright color. Petals come in many different shapes and sizes. Some petals are single and others are connected to one another.

In the middle of the petals are the stamens, which are thin and bend easily. They produce pollen. At the very center of the flower are the carpels. The seeds are produced here. For seeds to grow, pollen from the stamens must first enter the carpels. This process is called pollination.

Some plants don't flower at all yet still produce seeds. They are called gymnosperms, which means "naked seeds." Their seeds do not grow in carpels. Instead, the seeds grow in cones, such as pinecones. Some gymnosperms are short plants, and others are tall trees. Besides pine trees, gymnosperms also include fir trees and redwoods.

Another group of nonflowering plants, called tracheophytes, does not produce any seeds at all. Instead, these plants produce tiny objects called spores. Tracheophytes include ferns. It may look as if ferns have long branches with short leaves. These branches are actually called fronds. On the underside of a fern frond are small brown bumps, called sori. The sori protect cell cases where cells grow into spores. When it is warm, the cell cases dry out and break open. The spores are then carried away by the wind. A spore that lands where there is the right amount of heat and moisture can grow into a fern.

Mosses are part of a group of nonflowering plants called bryophytes. These plants lack roots, stems, and leaves. They are not able to transport water and nutrients within themselves. Each part of the plant must absorb its own water and nutrients. Most bryophytes live in wet and shady locations. Like ferns, mosses have spores rather than seeds.

Reading Time _____

Recalling Facts

1. The outer circle of a flower is made up of
   - ❏ a. petals.
   - ❏ b. sepals.
   - ❏ c. stamens.

2. Angiosperms
   - ❏ a. grow spores.
   - ❏ b. don't flower but do produce seeds.
   - ❏ c. are plants that grow flowers.

3. The seeds of gymnosperms
   - ❏ a. grow in carpels.
   - ❏ b. are spores.
   - ❏ c. grow in cones.

4. The word *gymnosperm* means
   - ❏ a. naked seed.
   - ❏ b. petals that are fused together.
   - ❏ c. bright color.

5. Redwood trees are
   - ❏ a. gymnosperms.
   - ❏ b. angiosperms.
   - ❏ c. ferns.

Understanding Ideas

6. From the information in this article you can conclude that
   - ❏ a. different types of plants reproduce in different ways.
   - ❏ b. all plants grow from seeds.
   - ❏ c. all plants have flowers.

7. If you are taking a walk and see a tree with cones on it, you know the tree is
   - ❏ a. an angiosperm.
   - ❏ b. a gymnosperm.
   - ❏ c. a sepal.

8. If you see a red rose, you know the red part of the flower consists of
   - ❏ a. sepals.
   - ❏ b. stamens.
   - ❏ c. petals.

9. Mosses grow best in rainy areas because
   - ❏ a. many ferns grow there.
   - ❏ b. they do not have any flowers.
   - ❏ c. they cannot absorb much water from the ground.

10. If you rub your finger across the stamens of a flower, you will likely
    - ❏ a. knock spores from the plant.
    - ❏ b. get pollen on your finger.
    - ❏ c. break open a cell case.

The Honeybee and Pollination

Flowers have special glands between their petals. A gland is an organ that produces a liquid. The glands between petals make a sweet liquid known as nectar.

Honeybees use nectar to make honey. They use honey for food. A bee flies from one flower to the next to collect nectar. It stores the nectar in a tiny sac, near its stomach, where the nectar turns into honey. At the same time that the bee takes in nectar, pollen from the stamens of the flower sticks to its legs. When the bee lands on another flower to get more nectar, some of the pollen on its legs rubs off on the plant's carpel. The carpel contains ovules, where eggs are formed. Pollination happens when pollen combines with an egg to form a seed. Seeds can drop from the plant and grow into more plants.

On each trip to get honey, a bee will usually go to the same type of flower. This is vital to the flowers. If the bee flew only from a flower of one kind to a flower of another kind, pollination would not take place. For example, a rose can't form a seed with pollen from a daisy.

One bee can visit up to 300 flowers in an hour. Now you know why bees are busy!

1. **Recognizing Words in Context**

   Find the word *vital* in the passage. One definition below is closest to the meaning of that word. One definition has the opposite or nearly opposite meaning. The remaining definition has a completely different meaning. Label the definitions C for *closest*, O for *opposite or nearly opposite*, and D for *different*.

   _____ a. unneeded

   _____ b. necessary

   _____ c. cluster

2. **Distinguishing Fact from Opinion**

   Two of the statements below present facts, which can be proved correct. The other statement is an *opinion*, which expresses someone's thoughts or beliefs. Label the statements F for *fact* and O for *opinion*.

   _____ a. Flowers have glands that make nectar.

   _____ b. Roses are the most beautiful kind of flower.

   _____ c. Bees get nectar from flowers.

3. **Keeping Events in Order**

   Label the statements below 1, 2, and 3 to show the order in which the events happen.

   _____ a. When the bee lands on another flower, pollen grains are transferred to the carpel.

   _____ b. The bee stores the nectar in a tiny sac.

   _____ c. A bee leaves the hive and collects nectar from a flower.

4. **Making Correct Inferences**

   Two of the statements below are correct *inferences,* or reasonable guesses. They are based on information in the passage. The other statement is an incorrect, or faulty, inference. Label the statements C for *correct* inference and F for *faulty* inference.

   _____ a. Pollen from a lily can pollinate a rose.

   _____ b. Bees carry pollen from one flower to another.

   _____ c. Bees do their work very quickly.

5. **Understanding Main Ideas**

   One of the statements below expresses the main idea of the passage. One statement is too general, or too broad. The other explains only part of the passage; it is too narrow. Label the statements M for *main idea,* B for *too broad,* and N for *too narrow.*

   _____ a. Flowers form seeds as a result of pollination.

   _____ b. Nectar comes from glands.

   _____ c. Honeybees pollinate flowers as they collect nectar.

Correct Answers, Part A _____

Correct Answers, Part B _____

Total Correct Answers _____

Waste and Recycling

Each year, people in the United States throw out more than 220 million tons of garbage. That's an average of about 2 kilograms (4½ pounds) per person each day. Figuring out what to do with so much waste is a huge problem. Most of the waste goes to landfills, where it is buried. This gets rid of the trash but can create other problems. Landfills can leak chemicals that pollute the land and water. Our landfills are filling up fast, and in some parts of the country we are running out of places for new ones.

Not all of our waste goes into landfills. Some of it is burned in big furnaces called incinerators. This can pollute the air. The rest of our waste gets recycled. To recycle means to make new things out of used things.

Paper is one of the easiest materials to recycle. Some kinds of paper that are recycled are newspaper, cardboard, and paper that is used in offices. When newspaper is recycled, it is mixed with hot water and turned into pulp. The pulp is mixed with a chemical that removes ink. The pulp is then used to make new paper. Recycled paper is much less expensive to make than new paper is.

About two-thirds of all steel is recycled. Some scrap steel is melted in a furnace and made into sheets. The sheets are used in making new cars, cans, and appliances.

About two-thirds of aluminum beverage cans are reused. The cans are crushed, then shredded and melted. Then they are made into large sheets. New cans are shaped from the sheets.

About a third of all glass is recycled. Almost all of this is from used glass containers. The glass is sorted by color into clear, brown, and green. It is melted and then formed into new glass items.

A small amount of plastic is reused. Plastic is harder to recycle than paper, steel, or glass. There are seven kinds of plastic used for containers. Each kind must be recycled separately. A number on the bottom of each plastic item tells what kind of plastic it is made of. Used plastic can be cleaned, shredded into flakes, and then melted into bits. These bits can be used to make new things.

Recycling is a good way to get rid of waste. Researchers are constantly looking for new, less expensive ways to recycle.

Reading Time _____

Recalling Facts

1. Each year, the United States produces about _____ tons of garbage.
   - ❏ a. 30 million
   - ❏ b. 220 million
   - ❏ c. 550 million

2. Landfills can pollute land and water because they
   - ❏ a. are filling up fast.
   - ❏ b. can leak chemicals.
   - ❏ c. burn waste in incinerators.

3. Most used aluminum beverage cans are
   - ❏ a. sorted by color.
   - ❏ b. never recycled.
   - ❏ c. made into new cans.

4. The seven kinds of plastic used for containers
   - ❏ a. can sometimes be mixed together for recycling.
   - ❏ b. can't be mixed together for recycling.
   - ❏ c. are always mixed together for recycling.

5. About _____ of all glass is recycled.
   - ❏ a. a third
   - ❏ b. three-fourths
   - ❏ c. an eighth

Understanding Ideas

6. From the information in this article, you can assume that
   - ❏ a. every kind of thing can be recycled.
   - ❏ b. recycling cuts down on waste.
   - ❏ c. most things can't be recycled.

7. One possible source of recycled steel would be
   - ❏ a. old cars.
   - ❏ b. dead trees.
   - ❏ c. brick houses.

8. One thing you might do to reduce waste is to
   - ❏ a. throw away old newspapers.
   - ❏ b. use disposable plastic cups.
   - ❏ c. make a used jar into a pencil holder.

9. The best way to get rid of waste is to
   - ❏ a. build more incinerators.
   - ❏ b. recycle more used items.
   - ❏ c. open more landfills.

10. The item that would be most likely to be recycled is
    - ❏ a. a plastic ketchup bottle.
    - ❏ b. a glass pickle jar.
    - ❏ c. an aluminum juice can.

Our Class Recycling Project

Our science class did a recycling project. Our teacher, Mr. Akerede, divided the class into three teams. Each team worked on one activity. My friend Cole was on the waste-exchange team. Members planned a kind of free garage sale. People brought things they no longer wanted or used, and they placed them on tables. Anyone who brought something to the exchange could take anything he or she could use. My mother traded a rake for a hammer.

I was captain of the No Trash Challenge Day. Our class challenged Ms. Johnson's class to see which group could get through a school day with the smallest amount of trash. My team took away all the wastebaskets and gave everyone a plastic bag to carry. All trash had to go into the bags. At the end of the day, we compared our class pile with the pile from Ms. Johnson's class. Our class won! My class had waste-free lunches. We brought our lunches in reusable containers instead of paper bags. We brought apples and oranges instead of candy bars with wrappers. We put the orange peels and apple cores on the school compost heap.

The news team made posters for the No Trash Challenge. They sent information on the waste exchange to the local newspaper. They wrote a newsletter to tell people how to recycle more.

1. **Recognizing Words in Context**

    Find the word *reusable* in the passage. One definition below is closest to the meaning of that word. One definition has the opposite or nearly opposite meaning. The remaining definition has a completely different meaning. Label the definitions C for *closest,* O for *opposite or nearly opposite,* and D for *different.*

    _____ a. reasonable

    _____ b. thrown away after one use

    _____ c. able to be used again

2. **Distinguishing Fact from Opinion**

    Two of the statements below present *facts,* which can be proved correct. The other statement is an *opinion,* which expresses someone's thoughts or beliefs. Label the statements F for *fact* and O for *opinion.*

    _____ a. Mr. Akerede's class won the No Trash Challenge.

    _____ b. The news team wrote a newsletter.

    _____ c. All schools should have a recycling newsletter.

3. Keeping Events in Order

Label the statements below 1, 2, and 3 to show the order in which the events happened.

_____ a. We ate apples and oranges.

_____ b. We brought lunches in reusable plastic bags.

_____ c. We put the orange peels and apple cores on the school compost heap.

4. Making Correct Inferences

Two of the statements below are correct *inferences,* or reasonable guesses. They are based on information in the passage. The other statement is an incorrect, or faulty, inference. Label the statements C for *correct* inference and F for *faulty* inference.

_____ a. A compost heap is a good way to get rid of fruit waste.

_____ b. Recycling things results in less trash.

_____ c. The only way to recycle things is to melt them down.

5. Understanding Main Ideas

One of the statements below expresses the main idea of the passage. One statement is too general, or too broad. The other explains only part of the passage; it is too narrow. Label the statements M for *main idea,* B for *too broad,* and N for *too narrow.*

_____ a. Mr. Akerede's science class did a three-part recycling project.

_____ b. Some classes study recycling.

_____ c. Mr. Akerede's class had a No Trash Challenge Day.

Correct Answers, Part A _____

Correct Answers, Part B _____

Total Correct Answers _____

Elijah McCoy, Inventor

Some people are curious about how mechanical things work. They have creative minds and like to build new things. They might watch someone do a job and think up a way to make the job easier or safer. These people are known as inventors.

Elijah McCoy was an inventor. His parents had been slaves in Kentucky. They ran away to Canada so they could be free. McCoy was born in Ontario in 1844. He went to school there until he was 15 years old. He was very interested in how mechanical things worked. His parents sent him to a school in Scotland. There he learned to be a mechanical engineer. Mechanical engineers design machines.

While McCoy was in Scotland, the Civil War was being fought in the United States. After the war, McCoy went home to Canada. Soon he moved to Michigan and got a job on a railroad. The managers of the railroad thought that an African-American could not be a good engineer. McCoy accepted a less important job taking care of trains.

McCoy kept the trains' steam engines working properly. He also oiled the moving parts of the train. This had to be done while the train was stopped, which was dangerous. When trains were stopped for oiling, other trains sometimes ran into them. It took a lot of time to oil the trains. McCoy invented a device that could oil a train while it was moving. In 1872, he got a patent from the government to make and sell his automatic oil cup. A patent is a piece of paper that shows who came up with a particular idea or design.

In less than 10 years, the automatic oil cup was being used in trains, ships, and many kinds of steam engines. McCoy moved to Detroit in 1882. There he thought up ways to improve steam engines. He also invented a fold-up ironing board and an automatic lawn sprinkler. In 1920, he started his own business. He invented devices and sold them. He used the earnings to improve his inventions. McCoy liked to show his work to children in his neighborhood. He urged them to go to school. He hired young African-American men to work for him.

McCoy kept on inventing for the rest of his life. At the age of 80, he got a patent for a tire. In all, McCoy had 57 patents for his inventions.

Reading Time _____

Recalling Facts

1. People who have creative minds and build new things are
   - ❏ a. college students.
   - ❏ b. railroad workers.
   - ❏ c. inventors.

2. Elijah McCoy was born in
   - ❏ a. 1844.
   - ❏ b. 1872.
   - ❏ c. 1882.

3. When Elijah McCoy worked for the railroad, he
   - ❏ a. was an engineer.
   - ❏ b. took care of trains.
   - ❏ c. invented steam engines.

4. Elijah McCoy invented
   - ❏ a. the automatic oil cup.
   - ❏ b. the steam engine.
   - ❏ c. patents.

5. Elijah McCoy started his own business to
   - ❏ a. make and sell his inventions.
   - ❏ b. sell steam engines.
   - ❏ c. build trains.

Understanding Ideas

6. From the information in this article, you can conclude that all inventors are
   - ❏ a. mechanical engineers.
   - ❏ b. educated in Europe.
   - ❏ c. creative.

7. You can conclude that Elijah McCoy
   - ❏ a. liked to do dangerous things.
   - ❏ b. liked to help other African Americans.
   - ❏ c. got rich from his inventions.

8. Of the following, the one that is not an invention is
   - ❏ a. plastic food wrap.
   - ❏ b. a can opener.
   - ❏ c. water.

9. McCoy most likely urged children to go to school so that they could
   - ❏ a. get better jobs when they grew up.
   - ❏ b. work for the railroad.
   - ❏ c. travel to Scotland.

10. If an inventor was walking her dog and the dog kept getting tangled in its leash, she would most likely
    - ❏ a. let the dog run free.
    - ❏ b. invent a new kind of dog leash.
    - ❏ c. scold the dog.

Why Do We Say That?

Have you ever heard someone say, "It's the real McCoy"? This means something is the best and not a fake. It is thought that this saying came from customers of Elijah McCoy. His device for oiling trains was so good that others tried to duplicate it. The railroads wanted McCoy's device and not a low-quality imitation. They wanted "the real McCoy."

Do you ever get so tired that you "run out of steam"? This saying comes from the steam engine. A steam engine has a fire that is made with coal. The fire boils water, which creates the steam that powers the engine. If a train uses up all of its coal, the water stops boiling and the engine runs out of steam. The train slows down and stops.

When you have to give someone bad news and you're not sure what to say, you might "beat around the bush." Rich hunters used to have their servants beat bushes and high grass to drive out the animals that were hiding there. If the servants beat around the outside of the bushes, the animals would often not come out.

Did you ever ask for a dozen doughnuts and get 13 instead? You got a "baker's dozen." In the Middle Ages, a person could be punished for selling less than he or she was paid for. Some bakers were not very good at counting. When they sold a dozen loaves, they gave out 13, just to be on the safe side.

1. **Recognizing Words in Context**

Find the word *duplicate* in the passage. One definition below is closest to the meaning of that word. One definition has the opposite or nearly opposite meaning. The remaining definition has a completely different meaning. Label the definitions C for *closest*, O for *opposite or nearly opposite*, and D for *different*.

_____ a. copy

_____ b. invent

_____ c. remove

2. **Distinguishing Fact from Opinion**

Two of the statements below present *facts*, which can be proved correct. The other statement is an *opinion*, which expresses someone's thoughts or beliefs. Label the statements F for *fact* and O for *opinion*.

_____ a. "The real McCoy" is something that is not a fake.

_____ b. Thirteen doughnuts are a "baker's dozen."

_____ c. The steam engine was one of the most important inventions.

3. **Keeping Events in Order**

Label the statements below 1, 2, and 3 to show the order in which the events happen.

_____ a. The coal runs out.

_____ b. There is no steam to run the engine.

_____ c. The train stops.

4. **Making Correct Inferences**

Two of the statements below are correct *inferences,* or reasonable guesses. They are based on information in the passage. The other statement is an incorrect, or faulty, inference. Label the statements C for *correct* inference and F for *faulty* inference.

_____ a. Many popular sayings come from real life.

_____ b. When we say things often, they become familiar.

_____ c. Old sayings have no meaning.

5. **Understanding Main Ideas**

One of the statements below expresses the main idea of the passage. One statement is too general, or too broad. The other explains only part of the passage; it is too narrow. Label the statements M for *main idea,* B for *too broad,* and N for *too narrow.*

_____ a. Hunters' servants used to beat bushes to drive out animals.

_____ b. Some old sayings have an interesting history.

_____ c. There are many old sayings.

Correct Answers, Part A _____

Correct Answers, Part B _____

Total Correct Answers _____

The Push and Pull of Magnets

There is an invisible force that can push and pull metal things. It sounds like magic, but it's real. This force is called magnetism.

People have known for many years that certain rocks have a pull on iron. These rocks contain magnetite, which is also called lodestone. Lodestone is a natural magnet.

Magnets are things that pull on some kinds of metal. This is why a magnet sticks to your refrigerator.

Everything is made up of tiny particles called atoms. Scientists think that each atom has a north pole and a south pole. These poles have opposite forces. In an object that is not a magnet, the atoms are not lined up in any particular way. The force of a north pole is balanced by the force of a nearby south pole. There may be a little magnetism, but it is so weak that the object won't attract metal. In a magnet, the atoms are lined up with all their north poles pointing one way and all their south poles pointing the other way. One end of the magnet now has the force of a north pole, while the other end has the force of a south pole.

A bar magnet is shaped like a long rectangle. The poles are at the ends of the bar. The opposite forces of the north and south poles attract each other. This pull from one end of the magnet to the other creates an area of force called a magnetic field. While north and south poles pull each other, two north poles or two south poles repel, or push away, each other. If you try to put the south poles of two magnets together, they will push each other apart.

Earth has magnetism. Picture Earth with a big bar magnet going through its center, with the North Pole at the top and the South Pole at the bottom. The magnetic north pole is near, but not exactly at, Earth's North Pole.

In a compass, the needle is a small magnet. The needle can turn freely. Its south pole is pulled toward Earth's magnetic north pole. The end of the needle that points north is sometimes red or marked with an *N* for "north."

Magnets have many other uses. Some construction cranes use them to lift heavy loads. Sound is recorded on magnetic tape. Many appliances have electric motors, which contain magnets.

Reading Time _____

Recalling Facts

1. Another name for magnetite is
   - ❏ a. lodestone.
   - ❏ b. magnetism.
   - ❏ c. atoms.

2. A bar magnet has
   - ❏ a. two south poles.
   - ❏ b. a north pole and a south pole.
   - ❏ c. two north poles.

3. A north pole and a south pole
   - ❏ a. repel each other.
   - ❏ b. attract each other.
   - ❏ c. have no magnetism.

4. In a magnet, the atoms are
   - ❏ a. shaped like a long rectangle.
   - ❏ b. not lined up any certain way.
   - ❏ c. lined up with their poles pointing the same way.

5. A compass needle always points
   - ❏ a. north.
   - ❏ b. west.
   - ❏ c. to the center of Earth.

Understanding Ideas

6. Of the following, the one that will not stick to a magnet is a
   - ❏ a. piece of iron.
   - ❏ b. plastic bottle cap.
   - ❏ c. metal paper clip.

7. If you brought the ends of two magnets together and they stuck to each other, you would know that the ends were
   - ❏ a. a north pole and a south pole.
   - ❏ b. two north poles.
   - ❏ c. two south poles.

8. If you laid a bar magnet in a toy boat and floated the boat on a puddle, the boat would
   - ❏ a. float without moving.
   - ❏ b. move in circles.
   - ❏ c. turn so that the magnet was lined up with Earth's north and south poles.

9. You can conclude from information in this article that
   - ❏ a. there are many uses for magnets.
   - ❏ b. magnets are usually tiny.
   - ❏ c. magnets are very cheap.

10. If you wanted to make sure you did not get lost on a hike in the woods, you would take along a
    - ❏ a. radio.
    - ❏ b. compass.
    - ❏ c. first-aid kit.

21 B   Making Magnets

To do this experiment you will need a small nail, a screwdriver, and a bar magnet.

For the first step, place the nail on the blade of the screwdriver. Unless the screwdriver is magnetized, the nail will not stick to it. If you find that your screwdriver acts like a magnet, find one that does not attract the nail.

In step two, place the nail on the bar magnet. Let it stay there for a minute.

In step three, pull the nail off the bar magnet and touch the nail to the blade of the screwdriver. What happens?

This time, the nail sticks to the screwdriver. While the nail was on the bar magnet, the magnet caused the atoms in the nail to line up with their poles in the same direction. This change caused the nail to become a magnet. As a magnet, the nail attracted the blade of the screwdriver. Bar magnets are made by putting a strong magnetic force on a piece of metal so that the poles in the metal line up.

Iron, steel, and nickel are ferromagnetic; that is, they are metals that are easy to magnetize. Some other metals can be made into weak magnets. Still other kinds of metal can't be magnetized at all.

1. **Recognizing Words in Context**

   Find the word *attracted* in the passage. One definition below is closest to the meaning of that word. One definition has the opposite or nearly opposite meaning. The remaining definition has a completely different meaning. Label the definitions C for *closest,* O for *opposite or nearly opposite,* and D for *different.*

   _____ a. pulled toward

   _____ b. pushed away

   _____ c. trusted

2. **Distinguishing Fact from Opinion**

   Two of the statements below present *facts,* which can be proved correct. The other statement is an *opinion,* which expresses someone's thoughts or beliefs. Label the statements F for *fact* and O for *opinion.*

   _____ a. It is fun to experiment with magnets.

   _____ b. Ferromagnetic metals are easy to magnetize.

   _____ c. In this experiment, the nail becomes a magnet.

3. Keeping Events in Order

Label the statements below 1, 2, and 3 to show the order in which the events happened.

_____ a. The nail was put on the bar magnet.

_____ b. The nail became a magnet.

_____ c. The magnet caused the atoms in the nail to line up with their poles in the same direction.

4. Making Correct Inferences

Two of the statements below are correct *inferences*, or reasonable guesses. They are based on information in the passage. The other statement is an incorrect, or faulty, inference. Label the statements C for *correct* inference and F for *faulty* inference.

_____ a. Some magnets are stronger than others.

_____ b. All metals can be magnetized.

_____ c. Some magnets can be used to make other magnets.

5. Understanding Main Ideas

One of the statements below expresses the main idea of the passage. One statement is too general, or too broad. The other explains only part of the passage; it is too narrow. Label the statements M for *main idea,* B for *too broad,* and N for *too narrow.*

_____ a. The nail sticks to the screwdriver.

_____ b. You can do experiments with magnets.

_____ c. You can do an experiment to make a nail into a magnet.

Correct Answers, Part A _____

Correct Answers, Part B _____

Total Correct Answers _____

A sister and a brother are walking in the woods. She hears a bird singing and sees raspberries on long thorny stems. She avoids the thorns while picking a raspberry. It feels bumpy. She pops it into her mouth and says it tastes sweet. Her brother hears a rustle in the bushes and sees a snake slither out, so he moves away.

Our bodies have sense organs that collect outside information. Our brains use this information to decide how we should react. The five basic senses are sight, smell, taste, hearing, and touch.

Our eyes are sight organs. The dark center of the eye is the pupil. In bright light, the pupil grows smaller so that less light can get in. In the dark, the pupil grows bigger to let in more light. Behind the pupil is the lens, which bends the light and focuses it on the retina. There, special cells send the image to the brain.

Odors come from tiny particles that travel through the air. Nerve endings in our noses sense these particles, and the olfactory nerves send the information to the brain. This is how we smell a skunk or a plate of freshly baked cookies.

We taste substances with our tongues. Our tongues have special groups of cells called taste buds. The front of the tongue tastes sweet things, and the sides taste salty and sour things. The back of the tongue tastes bitter things. Our taste buds need saliva to work. The more we chew and mix saliva with the food, the better we taste it.

Our ears are shaped like cups to pick up sound waves. Inside the ear, a canal directs the sound to the eardrum. The sound waves vibrate the eardrum. Three small bones behind the eardrum pass the vibrations on to the inner ear. There, they are picked up by the auditory, or hearing, nerve and carried to the brain.

We use our sense of touch to feel our surroundings. Nerve endings in the skin send signals to the brain. We can feel temperature, roughness, and wetness. We can feel different shapes, and we can feel pain.

Besides the five basic senses, there are as many as fifteen other senses. We have sense organs deep inside our bodies that sense things such as our weight and body position. We have a sense of balance. We sense when we are hungry, thirsty, or tired.

Reading Time _____

Recalling Facts

1. Our sense organs
   - ❏ a. decide how to react to information.
   - ❏ b. collect outside information.
   - ❏ c. are located in our brains.

2. In bright light, the pupil of the eye
   - ❏ a. grows smaller.
   - ❏ b. grows bigger.
   - ❏ c. bends light.

3. Odors are made up of
   - ❏ a. nerve endings in our noses.
   - ❏ b. substances we taste with our tongues.
   - ❏ c. tiny particles that travel through the air.

4. The front of the tongue tastes _____ things.
   - ❏ a. sweet
   - ❏ b. salty
   - ❏ c. bitter

5. Sound waves
   - ❏ a. are sent to the brain by the olfactory nerve.
   - ❏ b. cause the pupils of the eyes to grow bigger.
   - ❏ c. vibrate the eardrum.

Understanding Ideas

6. If you came into the kitchen where a just-baked cake was cooling on the counter, you would first use your
   - ❏ a. sight and hearing.
   - ❏ b. hearing and taste.
   - ❏ c. sight and smell.

7. You would use your retina to
   - ❏ a. smell a rose.
   - ❏ b. feel a rock.
   - ❏ c. watch clouds in the sky.

8. If you had been playing soccer all afternoon and your mouth was very dry, your sense of taste would be
   - ❏ a. stronger than usual.
   - ❏ b. weaker than usual.
   - ❏ c. about the same as usual.

9. Your olfactory nerve would most likely be involved if you
   - ❏ a. heard a car coming.
   - ❏ b. smelled a fire burning.
   - ❏ c. saw a frog jumping.

10. You can conclude from the information in this article that there are
   - ❏ a. only five senses.
   - ❏ b. 15 basic senses.
   - ❏ c. as many as 20 senses.

A Fish Out of Water

To do this science experiment, you will need crayons, two blank index cards, tape, and a pencil or wood dowel about 20 centimeters (8 inches) long.

Step one: Use the crayons to draw a fish in the middle of one index card. On the other card, draw a picture of a fish tank. The tank should be bigger than the fish.

Step two: Place the cards back to back. Tape them together along the sides, not along the top or bottom.

Step three: Slide the pencil or dowel between the cards. Tape the cards to the pencil so they are at the top of the pencil. The pencil should be in the center of the cards.

Step four: Hold the pencil between your palms. Spin the pencil while you look at the cards.

What happened? The fish looked as if it were in the tank. When your eyes send an image to your brain, it maintains the image for a short time. Your brain still saw the fish after it was gone. The same thing was true for the tank. The two images overlapped in your brain, so it looked as if the fish were in the tank.

A filmed cartoon works in the same way. The characters seem to be moving. What you really see is a series of still pictures. In each one, the characters are in slightly different positions. When the pictures are shown quickly, one after another, the characters appear to move.

1. **Recognizing Words in Context**

   Find the word *maintains* in the passage. One definition below is closest to the meaning of that word. One definition has the opposite or nearly opposite meaning. The remaining definition has a completely different meaning. Label the definitions C for *closest,* O for *opposite or nearly opposite,* and D for *different.*

   _____ a. keeps

   _____ b. erases

   _____ c. feels

2. **Distinguishing Fact from Opinion**

   Two of the statements below present *facts,* which can be proved correct. The other statement is an *opinion,* which expresses someone's thoughts or beliefs. Label the statements F for *fact* and O for *opinion.*

   _____ a. It takes a short time for images to travel from your eyes to your brain.

   _____ b. Cartoon characters do not really move.

   _____ c. Cartoons are the best kind of TV programs.

3. **Keeping Events in Order**

    Label the statements below 1, 2, and 3 to show the order in which the steps should be performed.

    _____ a. Spin the pencil.

    _____ b. Place the cards back to back.

    _____ c. Tape the cards.

4. **Making Correct Inferences**

    Two of the statements below are correct *inferences,* or reasonable guesses. They are based on information in the passage. The other statement is an incorrect, or faulty, inference. Label the statements C for *correct* inference and F for *faulty* inference.

    _____ a. Your brain can sometimes make you see things that aren't really there.

    _____ b. This experiment proves each eye sees something different.

    _____ c. If two pictures move back and forth fast enough, they will look like one picture.

5. **Understanding Main Ideas**

    One of the statements below expresses the main idea of the passage. One statement is too general, or too broad. The other explains only part of the passage; it is too narrow. Label the statements M for *main idea,* B for *too broad,* and N for *too narrow.*

    _____ a. There is much that scientists do not understand about the brain.

    _____ b. Cartoon characters do not really move.

    _____ c. A simple experiment can show how your eyes can trick you.

Correct Answers, Part A _____

Correct Answers, Part B _____

Total Correct Answers _____

Telescopes and Microscopes

Scientists often use tools to help them learn about things. Astronomers are scientists who study stars, planets, and the rest of outer space. One tool that astromoners use is the telescope. Most telescopes are optical. This means that they work by collecting light from stars. An optical telescope focuses the light to form an image. A lens at one end makes the image look larger.

Hans Lipperhey made one of the first telescopes. In 1608, he held one glass lens in front of another. When he looked through both, he found that objects looked much bigger.

Galileo was the first to use a telescope to look at the night sky. He saw that there were craters on the Moon. He studied the planets and confirmed that they revolve around the Sun. Until then, most people had thought that the Sun, the Moon, and the planets revolved around Earth.

The first telescopes worked by refraction. A glass lens was used to bend light to form an image. Light is made up of colors. A glass lens does not bend these colors evenly, so the image is not quite clear. In 1688, Isaac Newton made a reflecting telescope. It used mirrors to make a clear image.

Now there are large telescopes in many places on Earth. They are used to help astronomers find new planets and to learn more about the universe. The Hubble Space Telescope orbits Earth. It sends back detailed pictures from space. Much of what we know about the universe has come from what people have seen through telescopes.

Microscopes are tools that scientists use to see very tiny things. We can see things through a microscope that we can't see with just our eyes.

A simple microscope has one lens and can magnify an object up to 15 times its normal size. Compound microscopes use two lenses. Some can magnify things up to 2,000 times their normal size. Many microscopes sit on a stand. You can look down through a tube that contains the lenses. At the bottom is a stage that holds the object you want to see. A light enables you to see the stage. To focus on the object, you can move the lens closer to or farther from the object.

The most powerful microscope is the electron microscope, which is used for looking at cells. It can magnify an object to about 250,000 times its normal size.

Reading Time _____

Recalling Facts

1. Astronomers
   - ❏ a. make lenses.
   - ❏ b. look at evidence to solve crimes.
   - ❏ c. study objects that are in outer space.

2. The first person to use a telescope to look at the night sky was
   - ❏ a. Galileo.
   - ❏ b. Hubble.
   - ❏ c. Lipperhey.

3. The first telescopes worked by
   - ❏ a. microscopic magnification.
   - ❏ b. refraction.
   - ❏ c. compound lenses.

4. A compound microscope can magnify things
   - ❏ a. up to 15 times.
   - ❏ b. 80 times.
   - ❏ c. more than 2,000 times.

5. The most powerful kind of microscope is the
   - ❏ a. compound microscope.
   - ❏ b. electron microscope.
   - ❏ c. simple microscope.

Understanding Ideas

6. An astronomer would be most likely to
   - ❏ a. discover a new star.
   - ❏ b. examine cells under a microscope.
   - ❏ c. discover a new insect.

7. To look closely at a speck of dust, you would use a
   - ❏ a. telescope.
   - ❏ b. microscope.
   - ❏ c. mirror.

8. You would most likely use a microscope to look at
   - ❏ a. Mars.
   - ❏ b. the North Star.
   - ❏ c. a leaf.

9. A compound microscope is
   - ❏ a. less powerful than a simple microscope.
   - ❏ b. twice the size of a simple microscope.
   - ❏ c. more powerful than a simple microscope.

10. Microscopes and telescopes
   - ❏ a. help scientists answer questions.
   - ❏ b. make objects look smaller.
   - ❏ c. use colored light.

An Important Scientist

Robert Hooke was a scientist who lived in the 1600s. Hooke made the first compound microscope. He observed thin slices of cork. Cork is the light outer bark of a tree. Hooke saw that the cork had tiny holes, or pores, that were irregular in size and shape. They reminded him of a honeycomb. He used the word *cells* to describe what he saw. Hooke was the first person to see plant cells. Some of the other things that Hooke saw under the microscope were bird feathers, sponges, and insects. He wrote about what he saw and made detailed drawings. These went into his book *Micrographia*.

Hooke was also the first person to look at fossils with a microscope. Some scientists of the time thought that fossils were just stones with unusual patterns. Hooke looked at petrified wood, which is wood that has turned into stone. He compared it with rotten wood. He described how water that had minerals could turn dead wood to stone. He also looked at fossils under his microscope. Some fossils did not look like any living thing on Earth. Hooke figured out that some fossils were from extinct species.

Hooke also built a telescope and observed the planets. He studied earthquakes. He drew maps and designed buildings. He was famous for his work on clocks and watches. It is amazing that one person could make so many important discoveries in so many areas of science.

1. **Recognizing Words in Context**

   Find the word *irregular* in the passage. One definition below is closest to the meaning of that word. One definition has the opposite or nearly opposite meaning. The remaining definition has a completely different meaning. Label the definitions C for *closest*, O for *opposite or nearly opposite*, and D for *different*.

   _____ a. same

   _____ b. not regular

   _____ c. focused

2. **Distinguishing Fact from Opinion**

   Two of the statements below present *facts*, which can be proved correct. The other statement is an *opinion*, which expresses someone's thoughts or beliefs. Label the statements F for *fact* and O for *opinion*.

   _____ a. Hooke made the first compound microscope.

   _____ b. Hooke wrote *Micrographia*.

   _____ c. It is very hard to use a microscope correctly.

3. Keeping Events in Order

Label the statements below 1, 2, and 3 to show the order in which the events happened.

_____ a. Hooke observed thin slices of cork.

_____ b. Hooke made the first compound microscope.

_____ c. Hooke used the word *cells* to describe what he saw.

4. Making Correct Inferences

Two of the statements below are correct *inferences,* or reasonable guesses. They are based on information in the passage. The other statement is an incorrect, or faulty, inference. Label the statements C for *correct* inference and F for *faulty* inference.

_____ a. Hooke was an important scientist.

_____ b. Fossils can tell us about animals that lived long ago.

_____ c. Hooke thought that fossils were just unusual patterns in stones.

5. Understanding Main Ideas

One of the statements below expresses the main idea of the passage. One statement is too general, or too broad. The other explains only part of the passage; it is too narrow. Label the statements M for *main idea,* B for *too broad,* and N for *too narrow.*

_____ a. Robert Hooke made many important scientific discoveries.

_____ b. Important scientific discoveries were made during the 1600s.

_____ c. Hooke was the first person to see plant cells.

Correct Answers, Part A _____

Correct Answers, Part B _____

Total Correct Answers _____

The Life Cycle of a Tree

A tree begins to grow when it sprouts from a seed. The seed comes from a parent tree. There are two ways that trees make seeds. Trees that make seeds from flowers are angiosperms. When the flowers are pollinated, they produce seeds that are protected by coverings called fruits.

Not all of these trees have the kind of fruit you buy at the store. For example, the willow tree has a fruit you would not want to eat. Its fruit is a dry capsule-shaped object that bursts open and releases seeds. Willow seeds have fluffy fibers that float in the wind. They can float a long way before landing. Some trees' seeds are carried to new locations by water or animals.

Trees that do not reproduce by growing flowers are called gymnosperms. Gymnosperms have cones that form seeds when they are pollinated. The seeds fall from the cones to the ground.

On the ground, seeds germinate, or sprout, when they get the right combination of air, water, and sun. The tiny stem that grows is called a seedling. Seedlings may die if the soil is moved or if they do not receive enough water. A seedling that grows to a height of 180 centimeters (6 feet) is called a sapling.

As trees grow taller, their trunks get larger, and they grow new branches. This growth is caused by a group of special cells called the cambium at the inner surface of the bark. These cells divide to make xylem cells near the center of the trunk and phloem cells near the bark. Xylem cells carry water, and phloem cells carry food. As the roots grow, they take up more and more water and nutrients from the soil.

The leaves produce food for the tree through a process called photosynthesis. The tree uses the food for energy to live and grow. Leaves give off water into the air. If this water is not replaced, the leaves wilt. Water from the roots is pulled up to the leaves by the xylem.

Trees grow faster when there are more nutrients and water than when the soil is poor or dry. If you cut a tree trunk and look at the wood, you will see rings. Each ring was formed during one growth season. Wide rings form when conditions are good. A thin ring means it was a poor year for growth.

Reading Time _____

Recalling Facts

1. Trees that grow flowers are called
   ❏ a. seedlings.
   ❏ b. angiosperms.
   ❏ c. gymnosperms.

2. Seeds germinate
   ❏ a. on the ground when they get air, water, and sun.
   ❏ b. when they fall from the tree.
   ❏ c. when the fruits burst open.

3. The tiny stem that grows from a seed is called a
   ❏ a. root.
   ❏ b. sapling.
   ❏ c. seedling.

4. Tree growth is caused by the
   ❏ a. phloem.
   ❏ b. cambium.
   ❏ c. xylem.

5. A tree forms wide rings when
   ❏ a. growing conditions are good.
   ❏ b. growing conditions are poor.
   ❏ c. its roots spread out.

Understanding Ideas

6. From the information in this article, you can conclude that
   ❏ a. all trees grow from seeds.
   ❏ b. only angiosperms grow from seeds.
   ❏ c. only gymnosperms grow from seeds.

7. The life cycle of a tree
   ❏ a. includes many stages.
   ❏ b. begins when a tree is a sapling.
   ❏ c. ends with photosynthesis.

8. When it is hot and windy, leaves will
   ❏ a. lose less water than usual.
   ❏ b. lose more water than usual.
   ❏ c. send water to the roots.

9. Of the following, the one most likely to grow into an adult tree is a
   ❏ a. seedling.
   ❏ b. sapling.
   ❏ c. seed.

10. If you wanted to grow a tree from a seed, you would
   ❏ a. place the seed in a shady spot.
   ❏ b. plant the seed at the bottom of a deep hole.
   ❏ c. place the seed in soil in a sunny spot and water it.

Growing Applesauce

One morning, Mom looked out the kitchen window and said, "I wish we had an apple tree in the backyard." My sister and I agreed, so we went to a plant nursery. There we chose an apple tree that was about the same height as my mom. The tree was growing out of a big ball of dirt wrapped in burlap. We also bought a big bag of peat moss, which looked like black soil.

At home, Mom used the wheelbarrow to push the tree to the backyard. I carried the peat moss. My sister brought the shovel.

In the backyard, Mom handed me the shovel, pointed to the ground, and said, "Dig." I dug. Mom said the hole had to be as deep as the burlap ball was high.

When the hole was deep enough, Mom poured in the peat moss, and I mixed it into the dirt with the shovel. The peat moss made the soil more conducive to tree growth.

My sister and I rolled the tree into the hole. Then we removed the plastic string that was wound around the burlap, but we left the burlap. "The roots will grow right through it," Mom explained. Next, we shoveled dirt into the hole, about halfway up the ball. Then Mom brought the hose and filled the hole with water. When the water disappeared, we finished filling the hole with dirt.

As we admired our apple tree, Mom said, "Applesauce in about five years."

1. **Recognizing Words in Context**

   Find the word *conducive* in the passage. One definition below is closest to the meaning of that word. One definition has the opposite or nearly opposite meaning. The remaining definition has a completely different meaning. Label the definitions C for *closest,* O for *opposite or nearly opposite,* and D for *different.*

   _____ a. fertile

   _____ b. helpful

   _____ c. harmful

2. **Distinguishing Fact from Opinion**

   Two of the statements below present *facts,* which can be proved correct. The other statement is an *opinion,* which expresses someone's thoughts or beliefs. Label the statements F for *fact* and O for *opinion.*

   _____ a. Mom wished for an apple tree.

   _____ b. The apple tree was about as tall as Mom.

   _____ c. Apple trees are not easy to grow.

3. **Keeping Events in Order**

Label the statements below 1, 2, and 3 to show the order in which the events happened.

_____ a. Mom poured the peat moss.

_____ b. I dug a hole for the tree.

_____ c. My sister and I rolled the tree into the hole.

4. **Making Correct Inferences**

Two of the statements below are correct *inferences,* or reasonable guesses. They are based on information in the passage. The other statement is an incorrect, or faulty, inference. Label the statements C for *correct* inference and F for *faulty* inference.

_____ a. The family enjoyed planting their apple tree.

_____ b. An apple tree has to be a few years old before it grows apples.

_____ c. The children love applesauce.

5. **Understanding Main Ideas**

One of the statements below expresses the main idea of the passage. One statement is too general, or too broad. The other explains only part of the passage; it is too narrow. Label the statements M for *main idea,* B for *too broad,* and N for *too narrow.*

_____ a. We went to the plant nursery.

_____ b. My family planted an apple tree.

_____ c. Planting trees helps the environment.

Correct Answers, Part A _____

Correct Answers, Part B _____

Total Correct Answers _____

Animals that live in the wild must protect themselves from becoming meals for other animals. One way is to hide. Prairie dogs are rodents that live in "towns" made up of many burrows, underground holes used for shelter. If any prairie dog sees a threat, such as a hawk, it sounds a warning cry. The others pick up this cry, and all the prairie dogs hide in their burrows.

Another way some animals hide is by blending in with the background. This trick is called camouflage. The rose thorn hopper is a bug that looks like a thorn. It sits very still on a rose bush and faces the same way as the actual thorns. Arctic hares have white fur during the winter. They look like the snow that is all around them. When the snow melts, their fur changes to a speckled gray.

Some animals make themselves look big to scare away enemies. Puffer fish use water or air to blow themselves into a large ball. They also have spines, which make the ball seem more threatening. Cheetah cubs have long manes until they are three months old. The manes make them look bigger than they are.

Other animals protect themselves by being fast. A pronghorn antelope can run up to 90 kilometers per hour (55 miles per hour). Some lizards can run up to 30 kilometers per hour (19 miles per hour).

When an opossum is afraid, it plays dead. Other animals are good actors. If a person gets too close to a killdeer's nest, the mother bird makes a lot of noise and flaps its wings as if it is hurt. Then it tries to lead the person away from the nest.

A skunk does not hide or run but sprays an oil that smells terrible. Skunks are not the only ones to use scent as a defense; mink, snakes, and foxes do too.

Some animals have tough outer coverings. Armadillos have hard plates on their back and sides. When under attack, they curl up to protect their soft bellies. Many tortoises have strong shells.

Many animals fight to defend themselves. Sometimes they must fight members of their own species over territory. Bears and owls scratch with their claws. Some sheep and goats attack with their horns. Ostriches and kangaroos kick with their legs. Mice, squirrels, and wolves bite with their teeth.

Reading Time _____

Recalling Facts

1. Prairie dogs live in
   - ❏ a. nests.
   - ❏ b. burrows.
   - ❏ c. rose bushes.

2. Arctic hares protect themselves by
   - ❏ a. playing dead.
   - ❏ b. using camouflage.
   - ❏ c. using their teeth.

3. A killdeer protects its nest by
   - ❏ a. fighting.
   - ❏ b. running.
   - ❏ c. acting hurt.

4. When threatened, skunks
   - ❏ a. hide.
   - ❏ b. use scent as a defense.
   - ❏ c. run.

5. To defend themselves, some sheep
   - ❏ a. use their horns.
   - ❏ b. curl up.
   - ❏ c. strike with their tails.

Understanding Ideas

6. You can conclude from reading this article that
   - ❏ a. all animals run when afraid.
   - ❏ b. all animals hide when threatened.
   - ❏ c. different animals have different ways of protecting themselves.

7. You can conclude from the article that
   - ❏ a. pronghorn antelopes can run faster than lizards.
   - ❏ b. lizards can run faster than skunks.
   - ❏ c. opossums are slower than prairie dogs.

8. If you see a killdeer that makes noise and looks hurt, it is likely that it
   - ❏ a. is trying to keep you away from its nest.
   - ❏ b. has a broken wing.
   - ❏ c. wants you to help it.

9. If you see a skunk in your yard, you should
   - ❏ a. throw something at it.
   - ❏ b. stay far away from it.
   - ❏ c. chase it away.

10. If you were to "play possum," you would
    - ❏ a. pretend you were dead.
    - ❏ b. hide.
    - ❏ c. kick with your legs.

When people are dirty, they take a bath or a shower. Animals don't have bars of soap or bathtubs, but they do keep themselves clean. Many furry animals, such as dogs and cats, keep themselves clean by licking their fur. They also use their teeth to bite fleas and ticks or to pull out small clumps of dirt. Cats have rough tongues. When they lick their fur, it is almost as if they are being combed with a wet bristle brush.

Some animals that live in groups clean each other. Chimpanzees often groom one another. One chimp may groom an area that the other chimp can't reach.

Birds take baths to stay clean. First they wade in shallow water. Next they beat their wings. Then they fluff out their feathers to dry. Birds also take dust baths on the ground. It is thought that they do this to rid themselves of pests such as lice.

Even fish need cleaning. Fish have tiny animals called parasites that live on their scales and in their mouths. Parasites use other animals' bodies for sustenance. Some fish and shrimp live by eating these pests off other fish. Such fish are called "cleaner fish." Larger fish will open their mouths wide so that the cleaner fish can get in to clean.

Sometimes, one kind of animal cleans another kind. One example is the tick bird. It eats ticks from the backs of rhinoceroses.

1. **Recognizing Words in Context**

Find the word *sustenance* in the passage. One definition below is closest to the meaning of that word. One definition has the opposite or nearly opposite meaning. The remaining definition has a completely different meaning. Label the definitions C for *closest*, O for opposite or nearly *opposite*, and D for *different*.

_____ a. poison

_____ b. food

_____ c. fish

2. **Distinguishing Fact from Opinion**

Two of the statements below present *facts*, which can be proved correct. The other statement is an *opinion*, which expresses someone's thoughts or beliefs. Label the statements F for *fact* and O for *opinion*.

_____ a. Cats have rough tongues.

_____ b. Birds take dust baths.

_____ c. Chimpanzees are fun to watch.

3. **Keeping Events in Order**

Label the statements below 1, 2, and 3 to show the order in which the events happen.

_____ a. They beat their wings in the water.

_____ b. They fluff out their feathers to dry.

_____ c. Birds wade in shallow water.

4. **Making Correct Inferences**

Two of the statements below are correct *inferences,* or reasonable guesses. They are based on information in the passage. The other statement is an incorrect, or faulty, inference. Label the statements C for *correct* inference and F for *faulty* inference.

_____ a. There are many ways that animals keep clean.

_____ b. Cats are cleaner animals than dogs.

_____ c. Chimpanzees live in groups.

5. **Understanding Main Ideas**

One of the statements below expresses the main idea of the passage. One statement is too general, or too broad. The other explains only part of the passage; it is too narrow. Label the statements M for *main idea*, B for *too broad*, and N for *too narrow*.

_____ a. Animals clean themselves.

_____ b. Different animals keep clean in different ways.

_____ c. Birds take baths to stay clean.

Correct Answers, Part A _____

Correct Answers, Part B _____

Total Correct Answers _____

Answer Key

Reading Rate Graph

Comprehension Score Graph

Comprehension Skills Profile Graph

ANSWER KEY

1A	1. c	2. a	3. a	4. c	5. b	6. a	7. c	8. a	9. a	10. b
1B	1. D, O, C	2. O, F, F	3. 2, 1, 3	4. C, C, F	5. B, M, N					
2A	1. a	2. c	3. b	4. a	5. b	6. a	7. a	8. b	9. c	10. b
2B	1. O, C, D	2. O, F, F	3. 1, 2, 3	4. C, C, F	5. N, M, B					
3A	1. c	2. b	3. a	4. c	5. a	6. b	7. a	8. b	9. a	10. a
3B	1. C, O, D	2. F, O, F	3. 1, 3, 2	4. F, C, C	5. N, M, B					
4A	1. c	2. b	3. a	4. c	5. b	6. b	7. a	8. a	9. b	10. b
4B	1. D, C, O	2. O, F, F	3. 3, 1, 2	4. C, C, F	5. B, N, M					
5A	1. b	2. b	3. c	4. a	5. a	6. a	7. b	8. b	9. b	10. a
5B	1. D, C, O	2. F, F, O	3. 2, 3, 1	4. F, C, C	5. B, N, M					
6A	1. b	2. c	3. a	4. b	5. a	6. c	7. a	8. a	9. c	10. a
6B	1. D, C, O	2. F, F, O	3. 3, 1, 2	4. C, C, F	5. N, M, B					
7A	1. a	2. c	3. b	4. a	5. b	6. b	7. b	8. a	9. a	10. a
7B	1. C, D, O	2. F, O, F	3. 1, 3, 2	4. C, C, F	5. M, N, B					
8A	1. c	2. a	3. a	4. c	5. b	6. b	7. b	8. b	9. b	10. a
8B	1. C, O, D	2. O, F, F	3. 2, 3, 1	4. F, C, C	5. M, N, B					
9A	1. c	2. b	3. a	4. a	5. b	6. b	7. b	8. c	9. a	10. c
9B	1. D, C, O	2. F, F, O	3. 1, 3, 2	4. C, C, F	5. M, B, N					
10A	1. b	2. a	3. b	4. c	5. a	6. a	7. c	8. c	9. b	10. a
10B	1. O, C, D	2. O, F, F	3. 3, 1, 2	4. C, C, F	5. M, N, B					
11A	1. b	2. a	3. b	4. a	5. c	6. a	7. c	8. a	9. b	10. a
11B	1. C, O, D	2. F, F, O	3. 2, 1, 3	4. C, F, C	5. B, M, N					
12A	1. b	2. b	3. a	4. c	5. a	6. b	7. b	8. b	9. c	10. a
12B	1. D, C, O	2. F, F, O	3. 2, 3, 1	4. C, F, C	5. N, M, B					
13A	1. b	2. b	3. c	4. a	5. b	6. b	7. a	8. a	9. b	10. c
13B	1. C, O, D	2. F, O, F	3. S, A, S	4. F, C, C	5. B, M, N					

14A	1. a	2. b	3. a	4. c	5. c	6. c	7. b	8. b	9. b	10. a
14B	1. D, O, C	2. F, F, O	3. 1, 3, 2	4. C, C, F	5. M, B, N					
15A	1. a	2. c	3. a	4. c	5. a	6. b	7. a	8. a	9. b	10. a
15B	1. C, D, O	2. O, F, F	3. 3, 1, 2	4. C, F, C	5. M, N, B					
16A	1. b	2. a	3. c	4. c	5. b	6. c	7. b	8. a	9. c	10. b
16B	1. D, O, C	2. O, F, F	3. 1, 2, 3	4. C, C, F	5. N, B, M					
17A	1. c	2. b	3. a	4. a	5. b	6. a	7. c	8. a	9. a	10. c
17B	1. D, C, O	2. F, F, O	3. 3, 2, 1	4. C, C, F	5. N, B, M					
18A	1. b	2. c	3. c	4. a	5. a	6. a	7. b	8. c	9. c	10. b
18B	1. O, C, D	2. F, O, F	3. 3, 2, 1	4. F, C, C	5. B, N, M					
19A	1. b	2. b	3. c	4. b	5. a	6. b	7. a	8. c	9. b	10. c
19B	1. D, O, C	2. F, F, O	3. 2, 1, 3	4. C, C, F	5. M, B, N					
20A	1. c	2. a	3. b	4. a	5. a	6. c	7. b	8. c	9. a	10. b
20B	1. C, O, D	2. F, F, O	3. 1, 2, 3	4. C, C, F	5. N, M, B					
21A	1. a	2. b	3. b	4. c	5. a	6. b	7. a	8. c	9. a	10. b
21B	1. C, O, D	2. O, F, F	3. 1, 3, 2	4. C, F, C	5. N, B, M					
22A	1. b	2. a	3. c	4. a	5. c	6. c	7. c	8. b	9. b	10. c
22B	1. C, O, D	2. F, F, O	3. 3, 1, 2	4. C, F, C	5. B, N, M					
23A	1. c	2. a	3. b	4. c	5. b	6. a	7. b	8. c	9. c	10. a
23B	1. O, C, D	2. F, F, O	3. 2, 1, 3	4. C, C, F	5. M, B, N					
24A	1. b	2. a	3. c	4. b	5. a	6. a	7. a	8. b	9. b	10. c
24B	1. D, C, O	2. F, F, O	3. 3, 1, 2	4. C, C, F	5. N, M, B					
25A	1. b	2. b	3. c	4. b	5. a	6. c	7. a	8. a	9. b	10. a
25B	1. O, C, D	2. F, F, O	3. 2, 3, 1	4. C, F, C	5. B, M, N					

READING RATE

Put an X on the line above each lesson number to show your reading time and words-per-minute rate for that lesson.

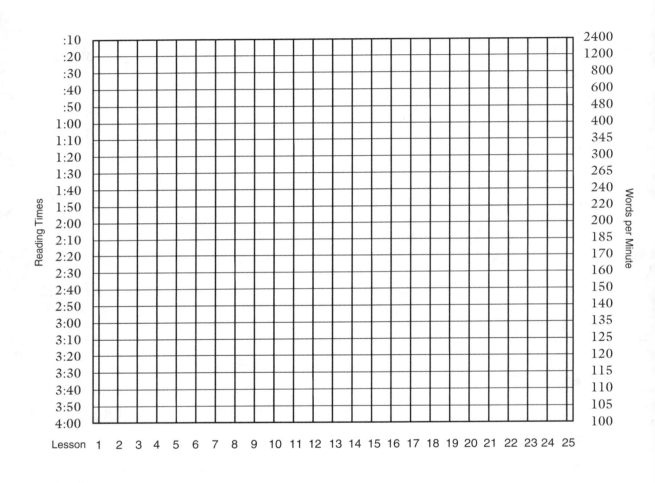

COMPREHENSION SCORE

Put an X on the line above each lesson number to indicate your total correct answers and comprehension score for that lesson.

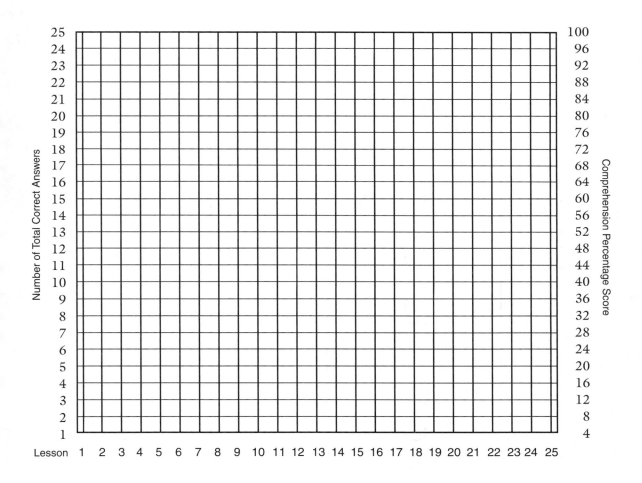

COMPREHENSION SKILLS PROFILE

Put an X in the box above each question type to indicate an incorrect reponse to any question of that type.

Lesson 1
2
3
4
5
6
7
8
9
10
11
12
13
14
15
16
17
18
19
20
21
22
23
24
25

Recognizing Words in Context

Distinguishing Fact from Opinion

Keeping Events in Order

Making Correct Inferences

Understanding Main Ideas